Photo by Yvette Wolterinck

According to her mother, Nanda was "born soon enough to get a taste of the Soviet Union, but late enough to not be brainwashed by it". Nanda found a passion for music in her early childhood, and she discovered the power of words through Latvian poets who rebelled against communism in the 80s. She's fluent in five languages and holds arts degrees from Latvia, France and the Netherlands. She writes and illustrates poems as @littlequibbles and previously used to work with her former partner in the Neon & Landa art duo, creating poetic, organic sound and light installations. Regardless of the season, Nanda loves eating jam straight from the jar.

This book is dedicated to all the children who grew up in the Soviet Union.

In memory of my father, cameraman Jānis Milbrets.

Nanda Milbreta

KOMMUNALKA CHILD

AUSTIN MACAULEY PUBLISHERS™

LONDON • CAMBRIDGE • NEW YORK • SHARJAH

A CIP catalogue record for this title is available from the British Library.

ISBN 9781398465046 (Paperback)
ISBN 9781398465053 (ePub e-book)

www.austinmacauley.com

First Published 2023
Austin Macauley Publishers Ltd®
1 Canada Square
Canary Wharf
London
E14 5AA

I was desperate to fix me and my family, and I was told to write. So, I wrote down every memory that crossed my mind. And it became a collection of illustrated childhood memories. The more I wrote, the better I understood. The better I understood, the easier I forgave. And when I forgave, I could finally heal. And when I drew, I could give it all meaning.

I would like to express my Gratitude to my siblings for being as they are and for inspiring me. And I'm forever grateful to my parents for giving me life and for exposing me to their peculiar sense of humour that now defines me too. I wrote this book because of my father, and I thank him not only for all the spicy details from his rebellious adventures that he felt ready to share with me during his final days but also for the stubborn character that I sure inherited from him. It helps me stick to the untamed paths of my wildest dreams. So, thank you dad and Rest in Peace.

Table of Contents

Part I

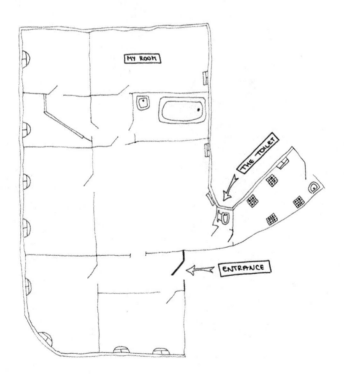

Meet My Father

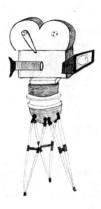

My mother and I were on our way home from the train station when we came upon a small crowd of pedestrians gathered around the statue of Lenin. We joined them to witness a man on a high crane shoot sparkles at Lenin's feet. He was detaching the legs of the statue from the pedestal.

There had been no official warning about the demounting of Lenin. My mother quickly searched for a coin in her pocket and rushed to the phonebooth down the street. She called my father, who was taking an afternoon nap.

'Quick, get all your film gear ready, they are dismantling the Lenin statue.'

My father ran as fast as he could with his heavy wooden tripod, his film rolls and a 35 mm camera. He got there just in time to set up his equipment.

He was the only person who filmed the notorious process of removing the Lenin statue in Riga, on August 24, 1991.[1] My father worked as a professional cameraman at the Riga Film Studio. His film materials were used for documenting Latvian events in the Soviet Union. Even though occasionally he

---

[1] To this day, his film material is used to portray the glorious last moment of Grandpa Lenin, who was hung with a metal chain. Latvians called the Lenin Statue the "Leninment".

worked as a photographer and as a director of photography for cel and stop-motion animation, documentaries were his greatest passion.

In my early youth, I rarely saw my father. He was always working and was often on the road for film shoots or to transport his film materials to Moscow. I had mixed feelings about his absence, as I knew that upon his return, my mother would report to him about my behaviour. Sometimes I spent days in fear, anticipating his punishment. When he got home, the time finally arrived – he laid me on his lap, pulled down my pants and spanked my butt with his hand.

'There you go! There you go! Do you understand now?'

This went on and on until I confirmed that I understood that what I had done was bad. My mother only did the spanking if my father was gone for a very long time. She couldn't bring herself to spank me by hand – instead, she used a belt. As she prepared to hit me, she closed her eyes and aimed for my naked butt. She mostly missed it, and I always felt that these were the lucky punishments, as hits to my back hurt far less.

When my father was home, we were not allowed to disturb him. If he saw us, he often shouted at us to "get lost in the woods". It must have been a common quote among partisans, the secretive armed groups that fought against occupying forces in WWII. Sometimes, when he was in a good mood, the whole family went to the park to feed the ducks. He made jokes, tickled me, threw me up in the air, carried me on his shoulders and told stories about his past. I loved listening to my father's adventures as a cameraman on film shoots for the Film Studio, or stories about his service in the Soviet army. As we were not allowed to have any pets, one of my favourite stories was about the mouse that moved into my father's previous house. He called him Mister Fyfkin. My father told me that all he had to do was make a special little sound and Mister Fyfkin immediately appeared in a tiny hole in the wall. Then he ran towards my father and climbed up on his shoulder.

He didn't talk much about politics but at home he was openly against the Soviet regime. He always admonished us to never share these conversations with people outside. Once he told me that before I was born there was a lot of censoring, because of which it was now forbidden to read, translate, distribute and own many books. Only the Party Elite – party members who had special privileges and rights denied to most people – allowed to own books that were censored, which otherwise had to be destroyed down to the last copy.

My father had a lot of courage and he rebelled against this system numerous times. When he told me the story of *Ulysses* by James Joyce, I didn't know anything about the writer or his modernist novel, but I was so impressed by my father's bravery that I never forgot the book. This literary work had been put on the censoring list, and so a good friend lent a copy to my father for a couple of days. My father knew what to do; determined to save the book, he photographed it page by page[2].

He undertook similar illegal acts at work in an effort to save the visual historical evidence of the regime. The so-called "Artistic Committee" would occasionally put out an order to destroy film footage that depicted censored content, such as traditional Latvian symbols. My father told me about one film that had to be edited multiple times to cut out all the shots that were taken in a room with white-and-purple striped wallpaper. According to the Artistic Committee, the colour combination was too reminiscent of the red-white-red of the Latvian flag. Being a patriot and hoping one day to see Latvia free again, in cases such as this my father took the brave step of preserving as much evidence as possible. If the order to destroy a specific film was issued, he first asked the girls at the lab to copy the film as a friendly favour. As "gratitude" he gave them a box of chocolates and liquor. In the Soviet Union, nothing could be achieved without a bottle of alcohol. This was called a "gratitude".

Then he exchanged the film rolls, preparing the film copy for the destruction. To avoid any suspicious behaviour, he swung the heavy can with the original film on his finger as if it were empty while he smuggled it home. Then he travelled to Moscow with the copy, where it was destroyed.

---

[2] The novel is 644 pages long, and the illegal Latvian copy was translated and published in the US.

Getting Under the Nails of the KGB

My father was a fan of Duke Ellington. When in 1971 Duke announced a tour with his jazz orchestra in the Soviet Union[3], my father, who was then in his twenties, had to find a way to attend the concert. In the Soviet Union, exclusive things such as this were only accessible to Party Elites and those who happened to have the right connections. As a cameraman, my father had shot film material for the Composer's Union, and that's the connection he used to get himself tickets to two of the Ellington concerts, one in Leningrad (now St Petersburg) and one in Minsk.

After attending the Leningrad concert, he decided to bring his camera to the Minsk one. During the show, my father stood up, walked towards the stage and started filming. When the security guard noticed this, he walked up to my father and grabbed his shoulder.

'Stop filming.'

He shook my father and repeated his warning.

'Stop filming immediately.'

My father knew that the security guard couldn't make any big dramatic movements without disturbing the concert and he used this to his advantage.

'Let's sort things out after the concert, when I'm done,' he said.

---

[3] This was later seen as a key cultural event within the context of US President Richard Nixon's attempts at détente during the peak of the Cold War. This series of concerts were met with great enthusiasm in the USSR, which stood in stark contrast to the Soviet government's disdainful view of jazz music as a symbol of American culture. For more information on the impact and implications of this event, see "Visions of Freedom: Duke Ellington in the Soviet Union", Harvey G Cohen, Popular Music, Vol 30, No. 3 (October 2011), pp. 297–313.

After the concert, my father started talking to Duke Ellington and was even invited to an after-party. A KGB agent followed my father all the way to Duke's apartment.

When my father returned to Riga, he received a warning from the KGB office for his reckless behaviour and he had to write a formal explanation of his actions. My father's excuse was that he "wasn't really filming but only testing the RIR screen". My father loved to provoke the authorities by using technical terminology that people outside of his specialisation didn't know to make them feel incompetent. This time he got away with only a warning on his record and an order to hand in the film material for destruction. My father asked one of his colleagues to make an illegal copy of his film from the Duke Ellington concert which he handed in personally in Moscow. This was of course accompanied with a little bottle of gratitude and a fake expression of shame and regret on his face.

In 1973, about a year and a half after this incident, another rebellious act by my father cost him more. At the Soviet Latvian Song Festival[4], he saw a KGB agent carrying a symbol that everyone recognised, an umbrella wrapped in the newspaper *PRAVDA* (the official newspaper of the Communist Party in the Soviet Union; the word means "truth" in Russian), trying to get a seat in the front row. My father chased him away, saying that the front rows were reserved for press-members, choir conductors and cameramen. The KGB agent left.

The next day my father was called in the director's office at the Film Studio. When he went to the office, next to the director sat that same KGB agent from the concert, who recognised him immediately.

---

[4] The Latvian Song and Dance Festival has been held every five years since 1873. This is one of the largest singing and dancing events in the world. Choirs and dance groups from the entire country (and from Latvian communities abroad) join a competition prior to the festival and based on the competition results they get selected to form a massive choir and dance group. Tens of thousands of performers unite on the stage, and tens of thousands more sing along in the audience. During the Soviet occupation, this event was renamed the "Soviet Latvian Song Festival".

'That's the one,' he said.

In light of the fact that he already had a warning on his record, standing up to the KGB this time cost my father his job. His camera was confiscated for a year and he was downgraded to "cameraman assistant".

Meet My Mother

My mother told me that she had blue blood and that she was an aristocrat. She didn't explain any details about her blood condition, but in some way, it was linked to eating small portions of high-quality food, exclusively with silver cutlery. She had relatives in America and Russia that regularly sent packages with delicacies, which made eating caviar a regular thing. She said that even in her early childhood she refused to use cutlery that wasn't made of silver. She was a fourth-generation Riga native and she was arrogant about it. When she argued with my father, she liked to remind him that in contrast to her, he had only moved to Riga in his early childhood. I found this remark very cruel, as my father's parents were living in Riga when his mother was pregnant with my father. WWII was coming to an end and they decided to flee the country. That didn't work out – they got stuck in the countryside, where my father ended up being born.

I learned from my mother that city people look down on those who come from smaller towns.

In my mother's passport, it said, "Nationality, Russian"[5], but she spoke very good Latvian, with just a slight Russian accent. When the Soviet Union fell apart, I learned at school to see Russians as our national enemies, to the point that I felt very ashamed about my Russian roots. If my mother spoke to me on the street, I waited to answer until nobody could hear us speak Russian.

All I know about my mother's ancestry is that she was raised by a Russian single mother, who in turn came from the household of a renowned Jewish surgeon, also working as a director of a hospital and a Latvian mother who changed her name to a Russian one because it gave her more safety during the occupation. When I first heard this story, I couldn't understand how exactly a

---

[5] To this day, people born in Latvia can have a non-Latvian nationality. Passports specifically state whether a person is a (non)citizen of Latvia.

Jewish father and a Latvian mother could create a Russian child, but the language they spoke at home was Russian, and that seemed to be enough to make the child count as "Russian". My mother never knew her father, but I can recall her once saying that he was a Russian soldier, which to my understanding makes my mother at most only one-third Russian.

I never saw any of her family photographs. When I once asked if she wanted to find out more about her father, my mother got angry.

'He was never there for me. Why would I want to know him?'

I never brought it up again.

From time to time, my mother dwelled in the past and told stories about her youth. She loved to talk about how when she was young, she trained in gymnastics, and how at sixteen, she started modelling on the catwalk. This is only speculation, but I'm guessing that it is because she grew up in an environment where appearance was so important that she became obsessed with being skinny – but then again, her preoccupation with weight could also be because of her aristocratic eating habits. Whatever the reason, nothing disgusted my mother more than obese people, and in her mind even people in a normal weight range were considered overweight. For years, my mother was convinced that I was overweight, although I just remember being hungry all the time. She pointed to the imprints on my ankles that were created by the elastics of my socks; this was enough evidence in her mind to prove that I was too fat.

In the '60s and '70s, my mother was a hippie but she swore she never did any drugs. She just loved the music – The Beatles, ABBA – and the bell-bottom pants. Some of her girlfriends dated marines, who travelled to the west and snuck LPs back into the Soviet Union and organised underground parties that my mother liked to attend.

My mother's biggest dream was to become a ballerina. But because she descended from a family of medics, she had no choice but to choose a more scientific profession. My mother ended up studying chemistry in Leningrad, and later she became a professional chemist in the chemical laboratory of the Riga Film Studio, the same place where my father was working. Both my parents took inexplicable pride in being a professional and they were disgusted by amateurs. Throughout my youth, they pushed me and my sisters to become professionals at something. In my parents' eyes, a person could only be a professional if they obtained a diploma. They constantly reminded us that things executed by amateurs were always done at a poor level, with no taste. If somebody happened to defend amateurs by saying that they are nice people, both my parents would always respond with the exact same sentence, 'Being a good person is not a profession.'

My mother got hired at the Riga Film Studio to develop 35 mm film negatives and look for defects in the filmed material. She often worked in the dark and even at home she avoided using bright lights. Her eyes were so well-trained at noticing the tiniest errors that she could spot a kopek coin on a dark street from half a block away. She took me to her laboratory a couple of times and I still have very vivid memories of her mixing chemicals in a chemical dish. As I witnessed the liquids change colour, I imagined that my mother's work was witchcraft.

My mother always hid her real age and never celebrated her birthdays. In my early teens, I once accidentally found a copy of her passport and was surprised to see that she was only three and a half years younger than my father. Once on her birthday I made the mistake of bringing her flowers – she refused to take them and locked herself in her room. For her, a birthday only meant ageing, although to my eyes she always looked very young.

My mother enjoyed dressing up nicely. She said she only had one item of everything – one blouse, one skirt, one pair of pants, one dress and one sweater – but that all her clothes were nice. None of her garments were bought recently but she knew how to take good care of them. Any money she had for clothes, she always spent on her shoes. She wore only high heels, "like any self-respecting woman". Considering that her body was always at least 5 cm off the ground, and preferably 12 cm, my mother was exceptionally graceful when navigating the cobblestoned city streets with a pram and grocery bags on her shoulders.

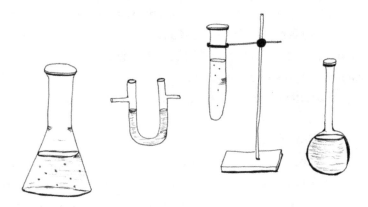

The Soviet Defect

My little sister once had a homework assignment at school in which she had to describe how our parents met. This is the story she heard from my father.

'Our father was on a trip to Estonia with his film crew. It was a rainy day. Their car was approaching a crossroad when suddenly a lumber truck appeared in front of them – the two cars collided. Seatbelts were not commonly used and so my father was launched through the front window. Their car somersaulted in the air several times. Out of reflex as a cameraman, and probably in shock, my father started filming. Soon after, he fell unconscious. The next thing he remembers, he was laying in the back of their car. He wasn't sure who put him there.

After the accident, my father's colleagues, and even his second wife, thought he had suffered brain damage, and nobody counted on him ever being able to return back to work. Sometime after the car accident he finally returned to work and went to the film lab, where he met a very pretty young girl in bright red pants and bright red lipstick. Her colleagues considered her good-looking, but dumb – my father seemed to be the only one who noticed that she was actually very intelligent and had a curious mind. The girl had already seen my father's film materials from the car accident and was the only one eager to hear his story. She wanted to know how it was possible to even survive such a collision, let alone document the immediate events after the accident.'

I've never heard my mother's side of the story, but I do know that she was very concerned about the standards of the Soviet society, and that she worried she would be seen as an old spinster. She was desperate to get married to alleviate pressure from society. They dated for about a year before getting married. The reason for postponing their wedding was my mother's requirement that my father finish his education and get his diploma. When my father wrapped up his studies, my parents finally set a wedding date.

In contrast to my mother's expectations, their wedding day was not the most beautiful day of her life. There was no white dress, no celebration, no guests and no wedding picture.

For her wedding day, my mother bought a beautiful, long satin skirt with a print of shiny ruby red and emerald green shapes. In my early youth, she wore it quite often, and I always gave her compliments, even though every time I realised right away that it brought up sad memories about her wedding day. My mother always told me that her relationship with my father was a "brak", an "unfortunate defect". The first time I remember hearing the word "brak" was when my mother tried to close a broken zipper on my coat. I only knew that the word meant "defect" and so my mother's complaint about her defect with my father made no sense.

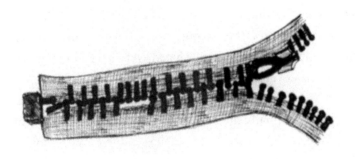

I later learned that the Russian word "brak" had two meanings, "marriage" and "defect". So, when I asked her why she voluntarily signed up for something broken, she didn't realise that I had been lost in translation. Her moments of complaint were monologues, where my role was to sit and listen. She always repeated that the defect was only still in place for me and my sisters and that she stayed for our happiness. She said that it was only thanks to her sacrifices that me and my siblings could build a bright future filled with opportunities. I had to promise several times that I was going to study hard, do well in life and ensure that my parents receive good care in their old age.

According to my mother's stories, for my father their defect was just another formality. On the day when my parents' defect became official, they exchanged rings and registered their partnership in the wedding registry that everybody referred to as ZAGS[6]. My mother never forgave my father for leaving for a work trip the day after their wedding day. They never had a honeymoon. There was no sparkle of love between them – I mostly saw them argue with each other. However, when me or my sisters asked why they don't divorce each other, they said that divorces only happen in bad families. We were a good family.

Three children were created as a result of my parents' defect. Most of the time I felt like a nuisance to the point that I wondered why my parents even bothered to have children. When I spoke about it to my mother, she explained that as a married couple they needed to contribute to society by growing the population. In the Soviet regime, the growth of the population was highly promoted and financially supported.

'What do you mean by growing population?' I asked her.

'Well, the first two children replace their parents, and the third one grows the population,' she explained. 'Honestly, I only wanted one child,' she added in a bitter voice.

I was her second child.

As my father wanted to be the only breadwinner in the family, my mother became an involuntary housewife. She hated every single moment of performing household tasks, and yet she was stuck in this lifestyle for ten years as she raised three children, only occasionally taking an opportunity to do some small jobs. By the time she was finally able to return back to work, the Soviet Union had fallen apart and the Film Studio had been closed down. When my younger sister was old enough, my mother felt urgency in regaining her financial independence. She completed a course in accountancy and briefly worked as an accountant. She even completed a whole new master's degree, possibly even two. The fact that I don't know the exact details of this is a result of us never really talking to each other.

It goes both ways – aside from some of my educational highlights, she didn't know much about my life either. I only know that eventually, years after the fall of the Soviet Union, my mother landed a job in a library but not just any library. It was at the tax office. In post-Soviet society, avoiding tax payments was such a common thing that my mother didn't dare to tell anyone that she worked at the

---

[6] This is an abbreviation for the Civil Registration Office, 'ЗАГС' (in Russian: отдел записей актов гражданского состояния). In the Soviet Union, institutions had long and complex titles, so it was common to use their abbreviations. Even when people spoke in Latvian, they often used the Russian abbreviations.

tax office. She was afraid that people would think that she would report them for avoiding their tax payments. By sticking to the title of "librarian", she felt like she would leave the impression of a trustworthy person.

Meet My Mother's Mother

In the periods when my father was gone for work, occasionally my mother would mention the cool guys she met during her study years in Leningrad. When she talked about them, her face briefly lit up. Her encounters from the past sounded promising and fun – for all she knew, she had missed a boat-load of opportunities. All those great people had moved on with their lives and gotten married. My mother often cried to me that because her own mother hated men, she ended up in an unhappy marriage with my father, as he was the only man who could handle her mother. Any romantic relationship that my mother tried to have got ruined.

One of my mother's most-repeated stories was how every time that she was about to go on a date, her mother instantly became so ill that she felt as if she was laying on her death bed. She demanded care for the final moments of her life. This strange behaviour might explain why my parents got married without her consent. My mother's mother continued acting like this even after my parents got married. My father recalled one specific time when she had called the ambulance because she was dying. When the ambulance arrived, my father heard the old woman yelling at somebody on the phone, so he decided to ambush her. He let the ambulance quietly enter her room. When she noticed the medics, she dropped the horn of the phone and in an amateurish theatrical manner she raised her hand to her forehead and fell into bed as if she had dropped dead.

When telling me these stories, my mother never referred to her mother by her name or by the title "your grandmother". It took me years until I finally understood that the stories about the character "my mother's mother" were actually about my very own grandmother.

In many folktales, grandmothers were portrayed as the kind, smiling ladies that sit in a rocking chair telling stories to their grandchildren and knitting woollen socks. In kindergarten and primary school, when I started interacting with other children, I heard them say adorable things about their grandparents, especially their grandmothers. Their grandparents were great at cooking delicious food, making jam and pickled veggies, reading and telling stories, knitting and sewing clothes. I didn't have any of that. For all I knew, my grandparents were non-existent. In my early youth, my biggest wish was to have a grandmother.

I Used to Think That All Homes Have Names and Ours Was Kommunalka

I spent the first nine years of my life living on Karl Marx Street in a gorgeous five-storey Art Nouveau building in the centre of Riga, right in front of the St Gertrude Old Church, around the corner from Lenin Street[7]. My parents told me that before communists occupied Latvia, the house where I grew up had belonged to aristocrats. Even though it had turned dark grey from layers of dust and was in urgent need of maintenance, the building radiated an exceptional beauty. For years, I admired the details of the facade. There were floating

---

[7] The central street that runs through Riga, from the old part of the city all the way to the outskirts. Over the course of history, the street has been renamed multiple times to align with the political situation in the country. After the fall of the Soviet Union, the street regained its pre-war name of Brīvības Street, which means "liberty" or "freedom" in Latvian. Karl Marx Street, meanwhile, regained the name Ģertrūdes Street, matching the name of the famous church.

decorative lines, flowers and devilish-looking heads. Our apartment was situated on the so-called "bel-étage", the floor right above the basement (but not quite at ground level). Compared to the rest of the building, the bel-étage had the highest ceiling. The basement of our house had full-size windows that were exactly half below and half above the ground. When I was growing up, I was always fascinated by the basement, but I never found out what it was used for.

My parents called our apartment "Kommunalka", and because of that I believed that every apartment had its own name. "Kommunalka" is Russian slang for the term "communal apartment". With the rise of communism, the population of Riga grew very rapidly due to the immigration of guest factory and care workers from other countries in the Soviet Union, causing a housing shortage. Kommunalkas were the communist way of solving this issue.

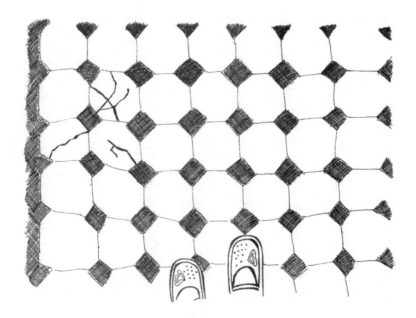

Depending on the size of the apartment, communal apartments were shared by at least two non-related families. Typically, each family had only one room of their own, and in that room, they did everything – they slept, they ate and they spent all their free time together. Everybody was allocated six square meters of living space. In our Kommunalka, as with all kommunalkas, the kitchen, bathroom and toilet were the shared, communal spaces. It was very typical to share one landline in communal apartments. The Kommunalka system also ensured that if your neighbour, or even a family member, showed any sign of subverting communist ideals or resisting the government, the secret police would be notified by a stukach. These were informants who turn in their friends, family and neighbours to the secret police, usually for a reward.

In our Kommunalka, there were six rooms, which were shared by thirteen people; my family, another family of five, a single mother with her daughter and an old woman. All our neighbours spoke Russian and knew almost no Latvian. My parents did everything they could to avoid contact with our neighbours, except for the single mother. If we accidentally crossed their paths, our conversations didn't go further than "hello" or "goodbye".

My Parents Could Never Be Sure When the Old Lady Was Listening to Their Conversation

My parents lived in a walk through room that had two doors. One door led to a tiny hallway that connected to the corridor, the bathroom and the room where I lived with my sisters. The other door led to the private room of the lonely old lady who lived in our Kommunalka. The only way for my parents to create some personal space was by placing a long cupboard diagonally through their room, as if it was a wall. The left side of the cupboard we called my parents' room and the space at the backside of the cupboard was the pathway for the old woman to reach her own room.

There was a lot of tension between my parents and the old lady, mainly because she always took a long time moving through that passage. My parents were convinced she walked slowly as a way to listen to their conversations. For a long period of time, our apartment had only one landline with four telephones, which made it easy to listen to the neighbours' conversations by carefully lifting the horn of the phone. Though the old lady wasn't reporting to the secret police, she was very eager to feed her own curiosity with any details she could glean about my parents' relationship. My father nicknamed her "Bushka". If my father pronounced the nickname in front of my mother, she became very agitated and commanded him to never do it again. My parents forbade me and my sisters from ever talking to her but they never explained the reason for this prohibition. It was clear to me that Bushka was an enemy of some sort, and if for whatever reason I happened to be left alone in my parents' room and I heard Bushka's slippers sliding along the floor on the other side of the cupboard, I would always report it to my mother at the first possible opportunity.

As I grew older, Bushka became more and more mysterious to me. When I started asking my mother more frequent questions about her, she finally explained that Bushka was her own mother.

'Why do you avoid your own mother?' I asked, very confused.

'It's complicated,' she said.

According to my mother, Bushka was categorically against my parents getting married (both my parents, but especially my father, used the word "categorically" to emphasise the importance of something). Of course, my parents were very uncomfortable with Bushka's unwelcoming attitude towards my father. My parents got married without Bushka's consent and their defect was followed by the eventual birth of my older sister. I learned from my mother that Bushka was such a selfish and unsympathetic person that she didn't give a single kopek to my parents, even though she knew oh so well that they were on the edge of starvation. Coldheartedly, she sat on a pile of money, and the only wedding gift she gave was a set of linens that my parents left untouched[8].

The other unacceptable thing about Bushka was that she was determined to get my older sister to herself. My parents were clear to her that they were categorically not going to give my sister away. When I heard this bizarre story about Bushka, I asked my older sister if she knew anything about it. To my great surprise, she said that she occasionally spent some time in Bushka's room when my mother had to do some things outside of Kommunalka, and what's more, that she liked it there. I was always very eager to see Bushka's room, and I was curious about the size of the money pile she was sitting on. It must have been huge; the ceiling of our Kommunalka was 4.15 meters high.

---

[8] Years later, when I was in my teens, my mother found them and gave them to me.

I only have one vague memory of once taking a glimpse into Bushka's room. I was on my way to my own room. The little hallway was dark. Someone grabbed my elbow and said that she wanted to show me something. It was Bushka. We both knew very well that this interaction was prohibited, but I was very curious, so I walked with her. She opened the door to her room and I saw beautiful antique furniture, paintings and a wall carpet[9]. To my disappointment, I saw no sign of the money that I imagined to be piled high right in the middle of the room. Instead, there was a big round table. When we heard my mother's steps approaching from the corridor, my heart started racing, and I rushed to my room as quickly as I could. My mother caught me halfway and said in an angry voice to not to hang around where I don't belong.

It wasn't until I started going to school that I became curious about the subject of grandparents. One of my classmates swore to me that he had four grandparents, comprised of two grandmothers and two grandfathers.

He's just showing off, I thought to myself.

'Oh yeah, what did you do then to get so many grandparents?' I asked.

By the confused look on his face, I could see he didn't expect such a question.

'Duh, I didn't have to do anything, I just have them,' he replied. 'They are mother and father of my parents.'

And then it finally struck me. Bushka, the mysterious old woman, was not only my mother's mother, Bushka was my grandmother, and my only grandparent alive. That evening I came home feeling like a detective that had made an exciting discovery and I was determined to reveal it to my sisters. When I told my older sister who Bushka was, she just said, 'Tell me something I don't know.' Then I turned to my younger sister.

'Did you know that Bushka is our grandmother?'

She shook her head and asked, 'Really? Is she?'

At least, I wasn't the only one who hadn't known.

Shortly after my amazing revelation, a strange lady approached my mother on the street and warned her to watch out for what her kids were eating. The woman said that Bushka had gone to a hex-lady to put a spell on a bag of candy so that she could lure her grandchildren to live with her. The only reason I know about my mother's encounter with this stranger is because my mother right afterwards asked me and my sisters if we had been finding candies around the house. My older sister immediately came forward to confirm that she had but she

---

[9] I learned much later that owning a wall carpet was a sign of wealth.

thought they were put into her coat pockets by my parents. I was very puzzled by this conversation. Did I really not notice any candies? That same day my mother checked all the pockets of our coats and indeed only found candies in my older sister's coat.

Over the next few days, late every evening my mother harvested the bewitched sweets. When she had collected a bag full of candies, she went to confront Bushka about it. I don't know the exact details of the conversation – all my mother told me was that my grandmother knew she had been caught and promised she wouldn't do it again. As a result, my older sister's cursed candy supply dried up. From this incident, I bitterly concluded that I wasn't my grandmother's chosen one. It also left me wondering about the kind of candies my sister had received, and more importantly, how many chocolate candies had I missed out on?

Meet the Baptists

In addition to my family, another family of five lived in our Kommunalka. This family was composed of Mother Sveta, Father Boris and their three sons, Kolya, Dima and Vladik. The boys were all about the same ages as me and my sisters. And because of our matching ages I was convinced that one day I would marry Dima and my sisters would marry the other brothers.

The head of the family was Sveta. My mother always pointed out how overweight she was, noting that during her three pregnancies she always ate for two. Sveta wore dresses with big roses that revealed her thick thighs, and she wound her dark brown hair up in a bun so tiny that it made her head look very small, accentuating the large size of her butt – at least that's how my mother told me to look at it. As I grew, my mother always warned me that if I ever cut my hair short my butt would look as big as Sveta's.

I didn't have any interaction with Sveta besides an occasional polite greeting. Sometimes I saw her in the corridor where she would often "hang on the phone", leaning her elbow on the commode, with the rest of the apartment at her back. To "hang on the phone" was an expression commonly used to describe somebody who holds lengthy conversations over the phone. This habit was very disturbing, as only one landline was available in our Kommunalka. While hanging on the phone, from time-to-time Sveta raised her left or right butt cheek, depending on which leg she leaned on more heavily. If I can believe the stories told by my mother, Sveta would spend hours hanging on the phone or cooking elaborate meals in the kitchen, making full use of Kommunalka's common rooms. When this mother of three boys cooked, savoury scents of delicious foods crawled from the kitchen into the rest of the apartment and I always secretly hoped she would invite me for dinner.

Sveta's family lived in the two rooms right at the main entrance of Kommunalka. Their doors had keyholes at three different heights for the three boys to peek through and report to their parents on the people entering

Kommunalka. Whenever we left or returned to Kommunalka, my parents rushed me past, but I always craned my neck to see if any of the doors to their living area were open. I was really curious to see how they lived. But the only thing that I managed to see were the thick carpets on the wall and on the ground all I could hear was the sound of a TV. Everything about this family was mysterious to me, and all I knew about them was what my parents told me, they were Baptists from Belarus. My parents also told me that these Baptists spoke the *wrong* Russian. When I asked what was so wrong about it, my mother told me in disgust that they didn't roll their "r" like proper Russians do and that their "g" sounded closer to "gh", which in her opinion was simply unacceptable.

I had no idea what being a Baptist actually meant, and when I once asked my parents about it, they said that it had something to do with the church. Officially, religion in the Soviet Union was non-existent[10], and in my family it wasn't practiced, but most of the children I knew were baptised. As I wasn't baptised, I found out from my parents (who were both baptised) that they had agreed to let us decide for ourselves when we grow older. When I asked why they didn't want to make this decision for us, my father said that he found the church hypocritical. In his opinion, it was ridiculous to listen to priests preaching, when in real life those same priests were doing bad things, often worse things than any atheist would do. In my parents' view, religious people could be more harmful than atheists, as all believers could simply ask for forgiveness. If they sat in a small box and talked about their weekly sins on Sunday, then on Monday they could start sinning again. These five people from Belarus were my only reference of how Baptists looked and behaved. This family lived a very social life and on Sundays they often invited their church friends to come over to our Kommunalka. As long as these guests were in the apartment, my sisters and I had to stay in our room.

In addition to distrusting Bushka, my parents also distrusted the Baptist family. My sisters and I played with the neighbour boys a few times outside, but my parents were never happy about it. They strictly forbid us from mentioning anything that concerned our family. On one of the rare occasions when we were

---

[10] Karl Marx described religion in his writing as the "opiate of the people", and the Soviet Union was officially atheist. The prohibition of religion caused a massive decline in the religiosity of people. In the Stalin years (until 1953), those who still practiced their religion were careful to hide it. Later, people could practice their religious activities at home and even in church, as long as they were not very open about it.

playing with the Baptist boys, Vladik gave me a piece of paper with a picture of Jesus. He told me that Jesus is holy. I had already seen the animated Bible Stories on TV, so I knew that when God talks to somebody, a ray of light shines down from the skies. Now that I had a picture of Jesus, I couldn't wait to see that light. That same evening, I put the portrait at my bedside and pretended I was asleep.

It was dark in the room. I squinted, waiting for the holy Jesus picture to glow, and a ray of light to shine down from the sky, but the magic light never came.

Welcome to My Room

As far back as my memory goes, I always lived in a big room along with my two sisters. But in reality, it wasn't all that simple. I once overheard my parents say that when my mother was pregnant with me, another family lived in our room. My older sister was only about two years old when my parents started the lengthy bureaucratic process of fighting for the opportunity to get more space than the walk-through room in which they were living with three people. This process re quired them to change their marital status several times. It took my parents three defects and two divorces to prove to the Soviet state that my mother and father belonged together and that they needed more than seven square meters of living area if they were to raise their children.

Our room was huge. It was filled mainly with my father's stuff – film equipment, books and artworks – and we were categorically not allowed to touch any of it. Many of my father's friends were artists and he found it important to support them. That's why the walls in our room were covered with art instead of carpets. From his friends, my father bought small-sized sculptures and paintings of full-sized naked women, not to mention a wide variety of still life's, landscapes, and countryside life paintings featuring tractors and people collecting potatoes. He also had a big personal library that took up one entire wall, from the ground to the ceiling. If anything was published as a series, he gathered the complete set. I loved reading books, but we never visited the library. For my father, it was important to own things and never to borrow anything from anybody else, not even a book from a public library. I guess he was categorically against the concept of communal property.

My sisters and I spent most of our time in our room without parent supervision. When I was about five years old, my father installed a speaker in our room and a little device with a microphone in my parents' room, through which my parents could communicate with us. My mother named this device "Matugalnik" (the Russian word for "megaphone"), and we used this word as a name for the device in both languages. With the help of Matugalnik, my parents announced when it was time to brush our teeth, or when they wanted to see us in their room. This was their way to look after us without needing to go into our room and without us being aware that they are monitoring us. We could never know when they listened, which was a great way for my parents to ambush us in the middle of an argument. When our parents punished us for arguing, we had to quietly sit in our beds. We came up with a secret, toy-free game where one of us had to read the titles of a book backwards, and the others had to guess the title of the book and point it out. Eventually the three of us got to know the names of a big part of my father's library backwards.

Our Kommunalka Playground

In my family, education always came first. We could only play outside if all our homework was done, and if the time and weather allowed it, and usually only on the weekend. There were very few playgrounds in the city and we rarely went to parks. Unlike many kids, who played on the street, we were only allowed to play in the yard of our building, and only while my mother was working in the kitchen.

The building where I grew up had an inner yard, with its main role as a parking place for the wealthier building inhabitants, such as party members and state employees. The absence of a swing, sand pit and a slide made us more inventive with the things that we could find. We played hide-and-seek amongst the cars and ran around on the ground, which was covered with old, broken asphalt and pits of hard sand. In the middle of the yard was a metallic grid with broken glass still stuck in its frame. This grid probably used to serve as a window for the basement area that was below our apartment and extended underneath the yard. From what I could see through holes in the glass, there was nothing in the basement apart from some leftover building materials. When we were bored, we threw stones and bits of asphalt through the holes into the basement. When it rained, we crawled close to the back of the cars to admire the rainbow-coloured stains that appeared underneath them. Then one day I noticed a big thin plate of rust ed metal laying on the ground.

When I pulled it up, it produced an impressive loud sound. I kicked it with my foot and was rewarded with the same sound again. It sounded just like thunder. Our yard was separated from the city by just a brick wall and behind the wall was the ever-busy Lenin Street. I was convinced that if I continued producing this sound, the passing pedestrians and the people waiting for the trolleybus would start looking for their umbrellas, thinking that rain is coming. I loved the idea of fooling the city, especially on sunny days.

Witches and the Cornman

When I was very small and it was time to go to bed, my father used to play bedtime stories on a record player. My sisters and I loved to listen to one particular story about a turtle.

But the thing I really looked forward to was listening to the gentle crackling of the needle on the spinning record. When the story finished, my father turned off the record player and then switched off the light. When we grew a bit older, we started listening to bedtime stories on the radio. In the evening, my parents alerted us through Matugalnik that it was time to tune into the radio. Since the dawn of the era of Matugalnik, turning on and off of the radio and the light became fully our own responsibility.

The task division in our room was done purely based on the practicalities of where and how we slept. The radio stood on a shelf above my little sister's baby bed, which is why we assigned her the responsibility of radio operator. She spent her nights in that bed until the age of seven and that's how long she continued operating the radio from the high-edged bed. One morning my little sister's long-time curiosity took over her – she found a screwdriver that fit and that morning she took the radio apart. When I saw the guts of the radio, I panicked. I feared we would never be able to hear our bedtime stories again, but by the end of that same day she had managed to flawlessly put the radio back together. It looked just like it did before and there were no orphan screws lingering around. The bedtime stories sounded just as good as before.

My older sister slept in the bunk bed above me, which meant that it was impractical for her to walk down the bed stairs to switch off the light and then climb back up in the dark. When the story on the radio was finished and my younger sister had turned the radio off, it was my responsibility to gather my courage, switch off the light and fight the monsters in our room on my way back to bed. The switch was all the way across the room. Once the light was out, I had to race back as fast as I could and I had to skip the last step before my bed. There was no way to get in my bed safely except by taking a long dive in the dark, because there were hundreds of witches under my bed whispering unrecognisable words. They stuck out their arms, trying to grab my ankles. Each time I barely managed not to get caught.

One time I slipped and hit my ankle against the sharp edge of the bed. It cut my skin but I had to stay quiet. If the witches smelled blood, they would get me with their greedy hands. Escaping the witches was just half of the challenge that I had to face every night. Once I landed in my bed, I immediately crawled under my blanket and lay down as still as I could. I breathed as shallowly and quietly as possible, so that the blanket on me wouldn't move.

Every night, Cornman snuck into our room through the top of the window. He landed on the edge of the top part of the bunkbed, where my older sister was sleeping, and then crawled along the walls. He always walked past my older sister so quietly that I don't know if she ever noticed him. Cornman was looking for me. One time I peeked through the hole in my blanket and saw how ugly and scary he was. His entire body was covered in blisters similar to the grains of corn and he had only one eye. The eye was big and green, and it was right in the middle of his face. In the morning, when it became light again, the witches and the Cornman were gone.

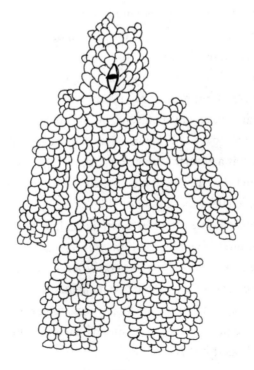

I Once Asked My Father Why the Foam Always Disappeared and He Said That the Dirt on Our Skin Ate It

The bathroom in our Kommunalka was big, which is good, because it was shared by thirteen people. There were four toiletry cupboards hanging on the bathroom wall, one for each family. The bathtub was antique. It stood on beautifully decorated legs that looked like animal feet. When emptying the tub, the water streamed down with a loud sound into a hole in the ground right beneath the tub, sometimes flooding the slippery stone bathroom floor.

The enamel coating of the bath was very worn out and rough. Once, while waiting for the tub to drain after a bath, I slid back and forth in the bath and rubbed off a strip of skin running down my spine. When my mother noticed how bad my back looked, she was worried that my kindergarten teachers would think that my parents had abused me.

In our Kommunalka, every family had the right to just one bath day per week. This may sound very limiting, but my parents assured me that there were many families who didn't have any bathroom at all, and for those people the only option left was to go to a public sauna. The Baptist family's bath days were on Fridays, and this was a cheerful, loud and steamy event. If we happened to brush our teeth right after they finished, we opened the bathroom window high up on the wall and watched the vapour pour out like clouds. The bathroom walls looked sweaty, the condensed water dripped down the ceiling and glided down the walls in thick and long lines. Even by the time we were done brushing our teeth, the mirror above the sink was still fogged up. When I once asked my father about the paint coming off the walls, he said that no paint could handle the high amount of steam the Baptists created on their bath day. According to my parents, this family was clearly unfamiliar with city life, which is why they used the bathroom "the peasant way", as if it was a sauna.

Our bath days were on Sundays. My father would fill the bathtub with very warm water. Sometimes, if he was in a good mood, he would open a plastic bottle with the word BADUSAN on it and pour a drop of soap in the bath. He said that he got the bottle in Moscow and that everybody in our Kommunalka was jealous about it. When he partially blocked the running water with his thumb, it shot out in a pressurised stream so that the soapy water foamed up. When the bath was full, one by one he carried us on his shoulder to the bath. If the water was too hot, we added a little cold water.

I loved to drink from the tap, as I had once noticed that it gave me a brief feeling of dizziness. Often, we sat in the bathtub alone to soak for what felt like an hour, until the foam in the bath had completely disappeared. Sometimes the water cooled down so much that we had to add more hot water.

If we felt we had sat there too long, we called out for our father. He once said that when we bathe, we shed our old skin. When he wrapped me in a towel and laid me on his shoulder to carry me back to my room, I took a glance at the water, hoping to see floating there a see-through peel of skin in the shape of my body.

Hairy Story #1

In my early youth, my hair barely grew – it was so thin and short that I was often confused with a boy. My parents were too poor to buy clothing and they gladly accepted clothes from their friends in Poland who had a son. Wearing boys' clothes didn't help me with my less-than-girly appearance.

Although I was still too young at this time to care about the state of my hair, my parents were really bothered by it. On one Sunday, my father came home with a special shampoo that he had been lucky enough to find in a shop in Moscow. Supposedly the shampoo stimulated hair growth. The first time he opened the bottle of this magical potion it filled the moist bathroom air with the lovely smell of freshly cut apples. He poured a drop of the shampoo on my head. While my father was closing the shampoo bottle, I could feel the cold drop slowly glide down my head. Just before it reached my eyelids, I closed my eyes. My father gently rubbed the shampoo in my hair. I enjoyed this massage while listening to the tiny, crispy sound of the shampoo bubbles popping in and around my ears.

Other Bathroom Activities

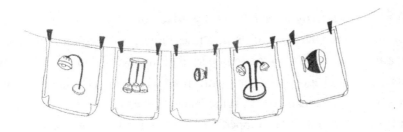

At night, while everybody was sleeping, my father was in the bathroom developing black-and-white photographs for lamp factory catalogues. I found out about his second job when I questioned him about the numerous stacks of lamp photographs in our room. Many of these photographs had edges that had curled up. My father said that photographs had to lay in a silver emulsion for the image to come through, after which he rinsed them in water and hung them out to dry.

'Paper curves in the drying process,' he said.

We Were a Good Family

My family was heavily affected both by a lack of money and by the national deficit of goods. Because of both these things, we couldn't always find toothpaste in the store, and for a long period of time we had to use tooth powder instead. It was packaged in a round, white plastic box. Each time I opened its lid, a very strong mint scent hit my nostrils. To use it, the toothbrush had to be wetted under running water and then dipped into the powder. If I forgot to shake off the excess water, the toothbrush picked up too much powder, which then turned into a big, wet lump. After my hygiene routine, I was left with the feeling of having squeaky sand between my teeth. No matter how well I rinsed my mouth, I just couldn't get rid of that sound.

We all went to our annual dentist appointments together because my parents wanted to be present while our teeth were checked. My father had known our dentist for decades; she was an old lady with thick glasses and a good sense of humour. In her world, fluoride tablets were holy. She praised them every time we met and swore that she herself committed to using them daily. One of our appointments was on a snowy winter day, and on that day, she told me that she had fallen on ice and despite her age she didn't suffer a single crack in her bones, all thanks to the fluoride pills.

My parents treasured her advice like gold. Instead of a goodnight kiss, they handed out fluoride tablets. And yet, despite this strict regime of daily fluoride tablets, both my sisters got cavities. I was proud that every one of my dentist appointments ended with compliments, until one day the unthinkable finally happened; I got a cavity, my only one. When the dentist noticed my father's angry eyebrow, she tried to make it sound like it was really no big deal.

'Oh, it's a teeny tiny one, I only need a minuscule drop of filling.'

I was frightened by my father's look and felt as if I had betrayed my family. I knew I had let him down and I felt ashamed. After the appointment and on the entire trip home, my father lectured me about the health sacrifices my mother had made for me. How could I be this careless and take it all for granted? How could I do this to them? To the family? My parents measured the quality of a family by the number of healthy teeth they had.

'Good teeth are a sign of a good family, and we are a good family,' they both constantly reminded me.

Both my parents had bad teeth.

Soviet Luxury

Because all thirteen of us had to share one toilet, each family had their own toilet seat that they had to bring with them when they went to do their business. After using the toilet, the family seat had to be stored away. I cannot recall how old I was when I saw toilet paper for the first time, but I remember very clearly that before that moment everybody used newspapers instead.

Going to the toilet was an event that required a preparatory ritual, the newspaper mashing. Through this process the paper turned softer and less slippery. This functional toilet literature was tempting for many people, who developed the habit of extensive reading sessions on the toilet, which in our Kommunalka sometimes caused lengthy queues. Once their deed was done, some people had the chance to wipe their butts with propaganda, while others used crosswords or weather predictions.

My parents always wanted to postpone our visits to the communal toilet and for a long time we used the white enamel potties in our room. I used a small blue plastic potty, which is why when I was very young, I thought that I peed green.

My Father Used To Tell Me
Our Family's Favourite Joke

If you visit the public toilet at the train station, then in return for the entrance fee, the lady working there will hand out one toilet paper sheet per visitor. But how can you use one sheet of toilet paper in a clever and efficient way if you have to take a number two?

Step 1 – Do your deed	**Step 2** – Fold the sheet in half.
Step 3 – Fold the sheet in half again.	**Step 4** – Rip off the corner of the fold and save it for later. Now you have created a hole in the middle of the paper.
Step 5 – Unfold the paper and put your finger through the hole.	**Step 6** – Wipe your butt with the finger on which you put the paper. **CENSORED**

Step 7 – To clean your finger, wrap the paper around it and pull it upwards.	**Step 8** – Use the corner of the fold that you saved earlier for cleaning out the bits that are stuck under and around your nail.

Meet Tanya Antonovna

In our Kommunalka, there lived a single mother, Tanya Antonovna, who raised her daughter Masha. All I knew about her was that she worked at the telephone switchboard centre and that through her work connections she managed at some point to arrange four separate landlines in our Kommunalka, which allowed phone calls to be more private for everybody. Tanya Antonovna had curly light-blond hair and friendly brown eyes that hid behind thick glasses in a big plastic frame. She always wore waistless dresses of stiff fabric that fell straight down on her tall and skinny body, so that it looked like she was wearing a bag. From time to time, if Tanya Antonovna had a difficult day, in the evening she loved to sip on alcohol. Most of all I remember her slightly shaky, nervous voice as she smoked a cigarette in the corridor.

She was always very loving towards me and my sisters. We liked her a lot. On rougher days at home, I imagined that this was not my family – these were not my parents and these were not my sisters – and that someday soon I would find my real mother, who was as sweet as Tanya Antonovna. When I played family-matching games with my sisters, my older sister was always quickest to pick Tanya Antonovna as her adoptive mother, leaving me and my younger sister with no choice but to pick Sveta, Bushka or someone else.

Masha was the same age as my older sister, which was probably the main reason my mother bonded with Tanya Antonovna. My mother told me multiple times that when Masha was a baby, she really loved carrots. Her mother gave her so much carrot juice that Masha's skin turned completely yellow. She was born with a heart defect. The girl was very skinny, her lips were blue, she had beautiful brown eyes and long curled-up eyelashes, but her dark hair was thin. Masha often fell ill, and as a result she lagged behind the regular school programme and had to be home-schooled. She was lonely and hoped for a sibling, and so Tanya Antonovna bought her a hamster. Masha often sought contact with us, and sometimes our mother allowed us to play with her, but never in our room.

Tanya Antonovna and Masha lived in a big room. All their furniture was set up along the walls – a bed for the mother and daughter, a wall carpet, a dining table, and a closet with their clothes – leaving the centre of the room free for a big carpet on which Masha often sat down to play. Masha had many nice toys. She got everything that she wanted, but she never acted spoiled. I remember once, when we played in their room, I was impressed with their massive radio with big knobs. The radio lit up when it was on. They also had a big TV. All we had was a small radio and a tiny black and white TV.

Sometimes Masha slid around the apartment in her slippers, occasionally gulping down jam straight from a large jar. I loved jam, too, but my mother rarely allowed me to have it. My mother said that jam was only meant for eating in winter, because in the summer there was enough fresh fruit and berries.

'But then why can Masha have jam in the summer?' I asked my mother.

'Because she's in poor health,' she answered.

In my eyes, jam was a delicacy.

If Tanya Antonovna baked pancakes, sometimes she gave some to us as well, with my mother's permission of course. According to my mother, the real fun in eating pancakes was in the amount. She said that the eggs in the pancakes of Tanya Antonovna made them too filling. If our mother ever made pancakes, she used only two ingredients, flour and water (and sometimes milk, but only in cases where she had some leftover that needed to be used). Her pancakes generally turned-out paper thin, burnt and dry. They were almost impossible to roll because they cracked and crumbled. To prove my mother wrong and give her a subtle nudge towards tastier pancakes, I once ate three of Tanya Antonovna's huge pancakes in one sitting. My mother thought I should be full after just one, but instead I asked if there was any possibility of having a fourth. I was determined.

'Not in a million years,' she said. 'A real lady has to eat the French way and leave the dining table with the slight feeling of hunger.'

Pam Barum Po Susekam

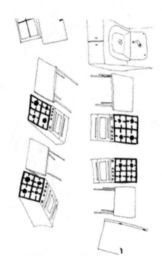

The largest room in our Kommunalka was in the centre of the apartment and it was shared equally by all four households. Everybody referred to this room as "the corridor" or Riga Tovarnaya (Russian for "Riga Shopping street"). Like a walk-in storage unit, it was filled with stuff that was arranged into maze-like corridors, creating a path that led to the toilet and the communal kitchen. Aside from many family belongings, including furniture that otherwise didn't fit in the family rooms, there also stood four fridges, one for each family.

The communal kitchen was big. There were four family stoves which stood on their own. My sisters and I were not allowed in the kitchen, with the only exception being when we wanted to play outside. Our mother would give us a signal when the kitchen was empty and then let us outside through the "black door".

'Why is it called the black door?' I asked my mother.

'Because in the times of aristocracy it was common for the apartments to have two entrances; the main entrance for the owners and the "black door" for the maid. The maid's entrance led straight to the kitchen, allowing her to bring in groceries unnoticed,' she said.

In my early youth, our family budget was extremely tight and our meals were very basic. To make ends meet, my mother become a true *ekonomka*. Growing up in a bilingual family where my parents didn't explain much, some things stayed a mystery to me and for some words I had to create my own interpretation. For example, in Russian, "ekonomka" means "housekeeper", but as I always heard my mother say that we had to "economise our financial resources". I concluded that this was the reason my mother became an ekonomka.

She took pride in her talent for being able to figure out the smartest way of spending money so that all the bills were paid and all the stomachs were filled. Throwing food away was out of question, even if it had already gone bad. We always had to eat until our plates were squeaky clean, and if there were any bits and crumbs leftover, that became my father's meal. When cooking, my mother didn't waste a drop. Sour milk was used for pancakes, old kefir ended up in *blinchiki* (little pancakes made of one tablespoon of baked kefir batter) and old cottage cheese in *syrnichki* (little pancakes made of cottage cheese batter). Sometimes my mother made a more royal version of *syrnichki,* if she could afford it, by adding raisins. When my mother made pancakes, she scrubbed out all the batter from the bowl and then cleaned the spoon with her finger right above the frying pan. When doing that, she would recite a common Russian saying, "Poskresti po susekam", which means "to scrub out all the last bits". I must have been very young when I repeated the saying for the first time because in my child language it became "pam barum po susekam" and my family adopted this saying right away.

An Ekonomka Sweet Bread Ball Recipe (Dessert)

1. *Collect old bits of dried out black bread and soak them for a while in a pan of water.*
2. *Strain out all the excess water and squash the bread into one mass.*
3. *Add some sugar and mix it in properly.*
4. *Start to roll the sweet bread balls in your palms, then leave them out to dry.*
5. *Serve the balls when they have dried out and hardened.*

Blinichki and Syrnichki

How We Killed the Worms

It was important for my mother to offer us a well-balanced diet. On working days, we got our state-funded warm meals in kindergarten and at school. During the weekend, we ate fixed meals. My mother couldn't handle the company of our neighbours in the kitchen and she avoided them. Her neighbour-free time in the kitchen was very limited, especially if Sveta was hosting guests. My mother was annoyed by the cooking scents produced by Sveta – she accused the woman of using herbs. My mother strongly believed that herbs are only used to mask the taste of products that have gone bad. To avoid our neighbours (which my mother spent a lot of time doing), she left pots and pans unstirred on the fire. Inevitably, the food was often so burnt that it was hard and black like coal. As a professional chemist, she knew coal for its properties as an absorber of bad substances in the stomach. Sometimes, after finishing our plates, our teeth were coloured black. My mother concluded that this was a positive thing.

As a child I was often hungry and hunger made me impatient. If my mother was very late with cooking, she gave us a common flour-based snack, bubliki, baranki, sushki, suhariki or pryaniki. It was only in retrospect that I realised that all these traditional Eastern-European snacks were a variation of dried bread. When she handed out one of the treats, she said that they were meant to "kill the worm" ("zamarit chervichka" in Russian). At that time, I interpreted this literally, as I didn't know that this was an expression that meant "to have a small bite before a proper meal". The thought of having a worm in my stomach felt unappetising and I couldn't understand why she was so calm about it.

'Do you have worms in your belly?' I asked my mother, who never ate any snacks.

'No, I don't,' she answered without realising why I was asking this question.

We didn't always get a snack when waiting for food and sometimes we had to wait a very long time for Sveta to finish cooking. My feeling of hunger grew quickly when the delicious scents seeped from the kitchen all the way to our end

61

of the apartment. On an empty stomach, I expressed my impatience by hammering my plate with a spoon. After a few broken plates, my mother had to take measures to preserve the family dishes. That's when we switched to enamel bowls that other households used for feeding their dogs.

Sushka

Suharik

Baranka

Pryanik

Bublik

My Mother Always Told Me
That Hercules Was Good for My Skin

On Saturdays, for breakfast, we ate oatmeal and we called it "Hercules"[11]. This was the worst morning of the week because my mother didn't know how to cook it properly. Only when she herself considered her Hercules to be a real failure would she bribe us with a spoonful of jam served in a little glass. My mother had two versions of failing at oatmeal; either it became solid, shaped exactly like the aluminium pan in which it was cooked; or it didn't cook equally, resulting in a burnt bottom with floating raw flakes of oats in a pool of warm milk, which, when it cooled down, got covered with a layer of yellow film. No matter the level of failure, throwing it away was out of question. A true ekonomka would never do that. I was traumatised by the porridge so many times that even on the days when Hercules was just right, the smell of it made me nauseous and the texture and taste of oatmeal triggered a gag reflex.

I told my mother many times that I wasn't able to eat it, and in return she always answered that, 'Hercules is good for your skin.'

When I grew up, she reminded me that I had her to thank (and Hercules) for my silky-smooth skin. She mentioned cooking that porridge as one of her greatest investments in me.

I spent my typical Saturday mornings staring at my Hercules plate for hours sitting alone at the table. Bit by bit I forced myself to swallow each bite of the porridge, telling myself that a finished bowl of Hercules would bring me closer to my favourite day of the week, Sunday. Only on Sunday mornings could we choose our breakfast. On those mornings, my mother entered our room to take orders. On the Sunday menu were boiled eggs, fried eggs or an omelette. For

---

[11] "Hercules" was a Soviet brand of oat flakes created in the 1920s. At that time, science had propagated the idea of healthy eating, and oatmeal was part of a healthy diet.

lunch, we ate meat. My mother generally didn't trust meat. She was obsessed with the idea that it's filled with bacteria and disease but she still insisted on feeding it to us. I could hear her hammer the meat in the kitchen to make it soft but that state was only temporary. When the meat was cooked, it burned on the stove for so long that it turned black and hard again. When cooking, she never tasted the food. The only "herb" she used was salt, but she used it in abundance.

The best thing about Sundays was our four-o'clock-in-the-afternoon snack, which we could enjoy while watching cartoons on TV. My mother called sugar the White Death and Sunday afternoon was the only time in the week when we got to eat something sweet. If one of us misbehaved, or if I got into an argument with my sisters that day, the dessert and the TV time were cancelled for all of us.

There Was One Soup That I Had Difficulty Getting Down My Throat

On weekdays in the morning, we had to rush to the kindergarten to have breakfast. The kindergarten served three meals a day; breakfast, lunch and an afternoon snack. This service was convenient for my mother, as she only had to cook on the weekends and could give us something small for a light dinner on working days.

In kindergarten, when it was time to eat, the children all tried to sit down in front of the pretty plate with an Easter bunny. Only after everybody had taken a seat and quietened down did the nanny walk around with a big aluminium pot to serve the food. Those who ate from the bunny plate were especially motivated to finish their portion.

I wasn't a picky eater, but there was one soup that I had difficulty getting down my throat, even when it was served on a bunny plate. It was milk and fish soup. When the soup cooled down, the milk formed a yellow film similar to that which covered my mother's poorly cooked Hercules. I tried to eat it before the film appeared, and if the film had already formed, I moved it with my spoon to the side of my plate. Sometimes the film broke up into bits and got stuck to my spoon. When I tried to get it off, some pieces broke off and went floating loosely around the plate. Swallowing those bits made me nauseous.

Jingle Bells, Jingle Bells, Perestroika Comes

I spent the first two years of my life at home, mostly alone in my room, while my mother was on paid parenting leave. My older sister was already going to kindergarten. When I was old enough for kindergarten, every morning and afternoon we travelled there and back home, taking my little sister along in the pram. My mother pushed the pram with both her hands while my older sister walked next to my mother. I walked on the other side, following her strict orders to hold onto her pocket. We were always in a rush. Often my steps were too small to keep up with my mother. Sometimes I caught myself not touching the ground with my feet and I felt as if I was flying. Eventually I would stumble and fall, pulling the fabric at the edge of the pocket down with me and ripping the stitch open. Fixing that stitch became a permanent part of my mother's daily routine.

The kindergarten was far away and we commuted by trolleybus. If we were on time, we caught the trolleybus with our usual driver. When he saw us running to the stop, he kept the front door open. During the ride, my sisters and I kept him company with singing. Our repertoire was vast and we even adapted it to the seasons. In the winter, we happily sang Jingle Bells. As we grew older, we changed the lyrics of the song to a version that we picked up from the older kids and we sang,

Jingle Bells,
Jingle Bells,
Perestroika comes![12]

---

[12] Perestroika was a political movement in the 1980s and early 1990s referring to the "restructuring" of the political and economic system in the Soviet Union.

I had no idea who or what Perestroika was. In my head, it was linked to the Russian word "stroika", a construction site, and I visualised a group of high cranes approaching our city like a herd of galloping giraffes.

Whenever we sang the Perestroika song, there were smiling passengers who seemed excited about it.

Once an old lady whispered to me, 'Keep on singing, my child.'

I'll never forget her face – it was wrinkled like mashed paper and her eyebrows seemed to be drawn on with a black pencil in a thin line. Her scalp shone through her puffy, purple hair.

Hairy Story #2

Once my father went on a work trip to Spain. I know this trip was very special because the borders to the west were closed and I didn't know of anybody who could cross them. I can't recall any of my father's stories about the trip – I only remember that my little sister was so small at the time that she crawled into my father's light brown leather boot and fit in it entirely, with only her head sticking out.

My father brought an unforgettable present back from his trip. It came in a pink paper package. My older sister read the name out loud, 'Hubba Bubba.' When we unpacked the wrapping paper, we found a fragrant rectangle that looked like a chess table with pink and black squares. My father explained that it was chewing gum, and that it was not meant for swallowing, only for chewing.

That was the very first time I saw and tasted a chewing gum and I spent an entire day doing nothing but chewing that one piece of gum. My older sister was always quick at figuring things out and soon she was blowing bubbles like big balloons. When she threw the balloon in the air, it fell straight to the ground. Then she picked it up and put it back in her mouth.

From time to time, I took it out of my mouth to inspect it. I was surprised to notice that the colourful chessboard had turned into a grey blob and after several hours it had almost entirely lost its taste and scent. After every close inspection, I saw my dirty fingerprints on the gum. When I put it back in my mouth and squeezed it with my teeth, a stream of cold saliva shot out of it. The chewing experience was so unique that I kept the gum in my mouth even when I went to bed.

The next day I woke up excited with a clear plan; I was going to chew the gum again. Only my mouth was empty. There was nothing. Did I lose it in my sleep? I looked for the gum in my bed but it wasn't there. I was so upset that I pulled my hair. That's when I realised that the chewing gum was still with me. It was in my hair. I tried to take it out but the soft lump was completely entangled. Crying, I ran to my father and showed him what had happened. He first tried to take it out with his fingers but in vain. He offered me two options, scissors or a comb. As I didn't want to lose a chunk of my hair and end up with a patch of short hair on my head, I asked my father to comb it out. My father combed my hair quietly, bit by bit collecting pieces of hairy chewing gum. Big silent tears were running down my cheeks while I watched the hairy gum land in the bathtub. I lost my chewing gum, and I was losing my hair. The skin on my head felt sore. I had to promise my father that I would keep this incident a secret from my mother.

The next day, before going to kindergarten, I asked my mother for a new piece of chewing gum. During the ride in the trolleybus, I enjoyed its sweet exotic flavour. When we arrived at the kindergarten, my mother asked me to wrap the gum in the trolleybus ticket to save it for that evening. I did exactly what she asked me to do (My mother obviously knew nothing about the sticky properties of chewing gum.) I couldn't wait to tell the other kids what was in my pocket.

'I have a piece of chewing gum, I have a piece of chewing gum,' I proudly said to one kid.

Others overheard me and ran towards me. In no time, I was surrounded by a group of curious kids and I felt important. With huge excitement, I unfolded the precious little ball made of the trolleybus ticket. To everybody's disappointment, the sticky lump was barely visible – it was spread across the ticket. The crowd around me dissolved very quickly leaving me alone with my embarrassment.

A Dangerous Trick

Once on a cold winter day, when everything was covered in snow, our kindergarten teacher wrapped all the kids up in their warmest clothes and sent us outside. When she saw my bare neck, she asked me what my scarf looked like. I told her that I didn't have one because in my family nobody wore a scarf. The teacher didn't believe me. She looked in a cupboard, pulled out an anonymous brown scarf, wrapped it around my neck and sent me outside with the others. I was upset that she didn't believe me and that I had to wear something that wasn't mine. I kept my neck stiff so that the scarf wouldn't touch my skin. It felt like a dirty beast was biting my neck with sharp teeth.

While we were playing, the teacher went inside with a kid that needed dry clothes. At that moment, a food truck drove up to our kindergarten. The driver parked the truck in the middle of the path and walked into the kitchen. Then one of the boys in my group told another boy that he could show everyone a dangerous trick. He went on all fours and crawled under the truck. He had disappeared and we were scared. But after a while he crawled out from the other end of the truck.

The trick was so exciting that more boys in my group wanted to try it. Soon after, the entire group of toddlers was crawling under the truck, including me. We were a bunch of kids totally unsupervised in the parking lot and we were high on the excitement of doing something naughty and not being caught.

The New Year Tree

To me, winter always felt like the longest season of the year. The temperature could drop down to minus 30° C, adorning windows with dazzling ice flowers. It dressed the world with a thick blanket of clean, bright snow, turning even the most forgotten and dirtiest corners of the city into a wonderland. Winter wasn't the right season for showing off your looks. The better you were wrapped up, the longer you could have fun. And in the winter every child knew how to enjoy ice and snow. There was just one restriction; don't eat the yellow snow.

When the snow was sticky, we made snowmen and had snowball fights. We looked for the longest icicles and broke them off to eat them as candy. I loved to hear the ice squeak between my teeth when I slowly chewed this icy treat. We slid on frozen puddles and laughed when we fell. If our mittens and knitted pants became heavy and wet, and if we found pieces of iced snow in our boots and sleeves, then we knew that we had enjoyed the winter to the fullest. When coming inside and taking off our soaked mittens, our hands and toes hurt from being frozen. We hung all our snowy clothes on the radiator and dipped our frozen hands and feet in a basin of cold water. Ironically, that was the least painful way to warm up.

There was little daylight in the winter, but my memories about winter remain very bright. Winter holidays were my father's favourite time of the year and he passed his love for it to us. It was also the only period when he seemed relaxed and was able to hang out with us at home. My father went to the market to pick out the most beautiful spruce. Then he carried it on his shoulder all the way to our home. My father believed that a proper New Year Tree[13] had to reach the ceiling. The high ceiling in Kommunalka made this a challenging task, which he solved by placing the tree on top of a black, antique desk that stood in our room.

---

[13] In the Soviet Union, Christmas trees and Christmas as a religious holiday were banned. In 1935, the festive home spruce tree was renamed the "New Year Tree".

We had to wait for a few hours for the branches to let go of the shape in which they were stuck when the tree was tied up for transportation. My father brought out boxes with colourful glass balls and other tree decorations, some even from his own childhood. I could tell from the nostalgic look in his eyes that he really enjoyed decorating the tree. I don't know why my mother never took part. We made snow on the branches by pulling a ball of cotton against the needles and we hung shiny silver angel hairs in the tree and on our own heads. When all the decorations were hung, my father clipped little candle holders on the branches and lit the candles. He watched them burn and always said that the one that burned out the quickest was a symbol of his life and that our candles would still burn long after his candle was out. It gave me a bitter feeling to hear that there was a future without my father in it[14]. He also told us that candles on the New Year Tree are a big fire hazard, and for that reason my father always stayed with us when they were burning, and he always double-checked that it was safe to leave them burn for a short while if he needed to step into another room. When the candles had burned down, my father blew them out.

---

[14] For most of my life, I lived in fear of losing my father, and for decades, I grieved for him, even though he was still alive.

Little Spruce

Winter holidays were always exciting and fun. I was free from school and could enjoy being with my family. At home, we baked a pile of gingerbread cookies. Along with my sisters, I pressed different cookie shapes into the gingerbread dough and put them on a baking sheet. Then my mother came to our room to pick them up and later she returned with the baked cookies.

The winter period was always filled with many concerts which added to the festive feeling. During the winter holidays it was very common to go to different festivities called "Little Spruces". These were not only for kindergartens and schools – workplaces also organised these events for the children of their employees. In the Soviet Union, Christmas could only be celebrated discretely within the family and so the main culmination of the winter holidays was the New Year's celebration. The winter festivities all took place around a spruce.

An old bearded man named *Ded Moroz* (Russian for "Father Frost"), often accompanied by his granddaughter Snegurochka ("Snow Maiden") wearing a long and shiny light-blue robe with a furry hat or crown shaped like a snowflake, would travel around the country carrying a big bag full of snacks and sweets that were usually packed in large felt socks or baggies. These gifts were always fragrant, a mix of scents made up of nuts, gingerbread cookies, candies, fresh cranberries in powdered sugar and later even mandarins. I was always especially happy if I got a bag with chocolate candies. Not only did they smell nice, they were wrapped in beautiful shiny paper with tassels, and it was very common to hang the wrapping in the tree as a candy-shaped decoration.

My father had several work connections so we would get to go to many Little Spruces. There was one mysterious night in particular where my father took me and my little sister to a place called "Little Pegasus". It was in the basement of a building and this unusual entrance made me think that we were visiting a secret place.

ough a maze of rooms. Everywhere on the walls there were
saw some children colouring at a table. A lady explained
tion studio for children and that it had some kind of
People sang songs or recited poems and in return they
esent. My father went on stage twice, and during one of these
ited a poem about a rabbit, for which he got a woven bookmark that
to me. For his second performance, he got an inflatable grey rubber duck
at he gave to my little sister.

The only time we ever went to church was on one winter night when my father took us to Mass at the St Gertrude Old Church. Even though the church was right in front of our house, it was the first time I saw its doors open. It was so full of people that we couldn't get any further than the entrance to listen to the organ music. It was a Christmas Mass in the period when the Soviet Union was about to collapse and government mandates no longer held the power they once did. That night I sensed a little bit of danger in being there but the night was peaceful.

In the 1990s, after 50 years of Soviet occupation, Christmas and New Year became equally important, and in my family, we began to find gifts under what we could now call the Christmas tree on both days. When I once mentioned Father Frost to my classmate, he wisely explained that Father Frost only existed in the Soviet Union. In the Republic of Latvia, the Christmas man had been reborn. I gradually learned that Christmas and Easter had some kind of link with Jesus. I had learned from Christmas songs that baby Jesus was born on Christmas Eve to Mary and Joseph but that he turned out to be the son of God and Mary was actually a virgin. If that wasn't confusing enough, on Easter I discovered that Jesus also had something to do with bunnies and eggs.

Life on the Dacha

In the summer, we lived in a wooden house in Jurmala, a beautiful seaside city on the Gulf of Riga. Russians called these types of summer houses a "dacha". Latvians also used this word, even though there is a proper Latvian word for them. For years, we spent our holidays in that dacha, the rights to which my father had earned for his outstanding work at the Riga Film Studio. Another four families lived in this dacha as well, all of them my parents' colleagues. The nicest thing about this house was that it was full of children and we were all friends.

The dacha was a beautiful wooden two-storey building that stood on a very big, fenced-off territory. There was a swing, a gazebo and a sand pit. The territory was very green and jasmine and lilacs were planted along the fence. My family had two big spaces, a veranda and a bedroom. We lived on the ground floor where the ceiling was about 3.5 metres high. Our veranda was on the corner of the house and it caught plenty of daylight. All of the windows had white crochet curtains. When we were indoors, the veranda was our main hang-out area. Here, my mother cooked on a portable electric stove, we dined, we did our hygiene routines, we played board games and we watched television on the little black-and-white TV that we took with us from Kommunalka.

There were four big beds in our bedroom. Our blankets were large and heavy; their colours ranged from green to brown. I later found out that these fabrics were used on film sets in the background. Our bedroom walls were made of veneer and we could easily hear our neighbours talk. They could hear us, too and unfortunately for them I was an early bird. At five in the morning, I was already up and singing my heart out. While my family pretended to be asleep, our neighbours banged on the paper-thin walls with their fists ordering me to shut up immediately. Other than that, we all got along very well.

Our dacha was only a ten-minute walk from the beach. On sunny days, we spent our time on the beach. My mother told us that in the morning and the afternoon the healthy ultraviolet sun rays helped us absorb vitamin D. Nobody used sunscreen. In my family, the way we protected our skin from the bad sun rays was by staying out of the direct sunlight but other people on our dacha spent entire days on the beach. They burned bright red, and after a number of days turned dark brown, and then their skin peeled off like the paint in our Kommunalka bathroom. Those who were shedding their skin competed with each other to see who could peel off a bigger chunk of skin.

My mother categorically forbade swimming in the sea. She was well aware that just a few kilometres down the beach there was a factory that dumped all its chemical waste into a river that flowed into the sea. Me and my sisters always looked on with great jealousy as other people took a swim. I had difficulty accepting my mother's theory – if it were true, wouldn't other people also avoid swimming in water that's filled with bad chemicals? On hot days, the beach was covered with empty towels and everybody was in the sea. We sometimes followed our friends into the sea, making sure that the water didn't reach higher than our knees. If children running by splashed us, we got grounded and had to return to our dacha immediately. Once I was splashed by a kid so badly that an allergic reaction occurred on my cheek which looked like burn blisters. That's how sensitive my silky skin was to the factory chemicals.

In the evening, I sometimes joined my mother for a walk on the beach and I always kept an eye out for beach treasures like seashells, feathers and round pieces of wood, or in rare cases a tiny piece of amber. Then one day a radio reporter made an emergency announcement stating that several people had received high-degree burns after collecting amber-like stones that turned out to be phosphorus from the army. From then on, my mother forbade touching any stone-like thing on the beach. During our walks we also looked out for empty beer bottles. When we brought them to the recycling place, we got some kopeks in return, which was our pocket money.

Meet Kostia

One of my summer friends from the dacha was Kostia, a boy with curly hair and thick glasses that made his eyes look like tiny needle points. Kostia was passionate about astronomy and math. His mother always called him by his full name, Konstantin, and told everybody that he's an intellectual. She praised him so much that I always felt stupid and worthless. Both of them spent their evenings sitting on the bench in the garden of our dacha figuring out riddles and formulas or reading books about astronomy.

I was Kostia's one-sided love. When he was free to play, he followed me everywhere.

Every time he saw me from afar, he would shout, 'Panda-Vanda-Allamanda, Panda-Vanda-Allamanda!'

He came up with this nickname and I hated it. No matter how much I begged him to leave me alone, he always stuck around. I was very annoyed that he was in love with me.

Once a kid on our dacha came up with a game where we had to split in pairs, and whenever we had to divide in couples, Kostia insisted on being paired up with me. The new game was simple; one person in each pair was "the puller" and they had to drag the other person to a place that was assigned to them. Our pair was assigned to the gazebo.

'I want to be the puller!' exclaimed Kostia.

When the game started, I used my entire weight to act like a heavy potato bag, but despite all my resistance, we were getting closer and closer to the gazebo. And then Kostia stepped into it. At that point, I was around the corner from the entrance of the gazebo. Kostia was holding onto my hand with his stretched arms and used all his strength to pull me in. Neither of us noticed that the head of a nail was sticking out of the gazebo's wooden frame. His pulling and my resistance to it caused so much friction that the head of the nail cut through my skin. The moment I felt that, I screamed, 'Stop! Stop!' but Kostia thought I didn't want to be pulled into the gazebo and in the excitement of the moment, knowing he was about to win the game, he pulled me even harder. I felt the nail sink deeper in my skin, further opening the wound on my arm. Kostia wouldn't let go. It took me some time to realise that it was better to surrender to Kostia's efforts so that it was over as quickly as possible.

He dragged me in the gazebo like his prey and he shouted at the top of his lungs, 'I won, I won, I won!'

I was crying but Kostia kept laughing.

'Look at what you did to me.' I sobbed. All the other kids gathered in the gazebo and I showed them the deep open wound on my arm. To my surprise it was barely bleeding.

'Look at the colour! Why is it light blue?' I asked, confused.

'It's your muscle,' said an older kid.

When everyone's eyes turned towards Kostia, he ran home without saying a word.

There was another silly game that we played but this one we played only once. One of the kids told us that Kostia's father didn't wear underpants. The man had a full beard, hairy legs and he always walked around in very short jean shorts. One time when Kostia's father was standing near the swing on which I was swinging, I wanted to use the opportunity to peek at his pants from below, to check if the rumour was true. All the kids quickly gathered around the swing with the same idea in mind. They squatted down and waddled closer and closer to Kostia's father, until he was surrounded by a swarm of squatting children. It all became so weird and awkward that he left, confused, and we never found out if he did or did not wear underpants.

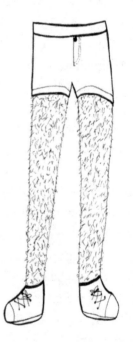

The Symphony of Slugs

On colder summer days, the kids from our dacha gathered in the gazebo to read scary stories and play board games. On rainy days, we went snail hunting so that we could set up a snail farm on the benches of the gazebo. For these snails, we built our idea of comfortable nests and we took care of them by supplying them daily with fresh leaves. We watched their red mouths open and their little white teeth take bites from the leaves. We touched their tentacles and watched them shrink and then stretch out again. We inspected their shiny traces and their spiralling, looping poop. But most of all we were happy to find their eggs, which after a while became tiny, almost see-through baby snails.

After a heavy rain on warm summer days, I loved running around with bare feet and stepping into the puddles. When the sun was shining, the ground and the roofs released moisture from the rainwater creating such an abundant amount of vapour that I thought everything was on fire. This rare and impressive steamy sight came with rhythmical "patsss" and "plaksh" beats. I looked around trying to see what was causing these sounds. And I was disgusted when I found out that I was listening to the suicide song of big black slugs. They were falling off the branches of the leafy trees and landing on the hard tiles of our garden. There were so many of them that the hard ground looked like a war zone, covered with burst slug bodies and exposed slug guts. There was nothing cute about the slugs.

My Mother Always Told Me That Aristocrats Speak French

By the age of six, I was growing so fast that I had already outgrown my older sister. My parents were afraid that I would be bullied at school if I waited for another year to start, so they registered me a year early for the school entrance exam. At the exam, my reading speed was determined to be "insufficient". After negotiations and promises that I would practice reading throughout the summer, the school director offered me a second chance to take the test at the end of the summer. I spent the whole holiday period with my nose in books. In 1989, I enrolled in first grade at Henri Barbusse 11th high school. Alongside my classmates Sonya and Ella, I was one of the three youngest pupils in my class but at least I was of average height.

The new study year started on September 1. On this first day of school, students gathered in front of the school to listen to a celebratory opening speech by the school director followed by the Soviet and French anthems. The most excellent pupil of the school rang a little bell, symbolically opening the new school year. That day, all the students wore the festive version of their Soviet uniform with white knee-height socks that had hanging tassels of yarn. At the end of the celebratory opening, students gave flowers to their teacher[15].

Henri Barbusse 11th high school was specialised in the French language; it was named after a French novelist and member of the French Communist party. There were Latvian and Russian "streams" of pupils in my school. Latvian kids got their education in Latvian and Russian kids in Russian[16]. We all had classes in the same building. The two streams coexisted without interference, like they lived in two parallel worlds. The only interaction between the two streams, which was a major exception, occurred in the Physical Education lessons (called "Fizra" in Russian, short for "Fizkultura"), when we had to share the sport hall. When this happened, the teach er made the two classes play a game against each other and those games always had a very nationalistic tone. It wasn't about one class winning over the other, it was about the Russians beating the Latvians or vice versa.

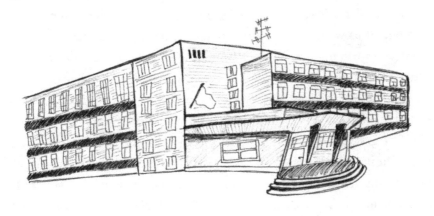

---

[15] To this day, the new study year always starts on September 1, even if it falls on the weekend. The tradition of offering flowers every year on the first day of school has also been preserved.

[16] By the time I graduated from primary school, there was no more separation based on nationality. If Russian children enrolled in my school, they received their education in Latvian.

Strive for Perfection

As each lesson started we stood behind our desks waiting for the teacher to come into the classroom and say, 'Good morning, class.'

Then we unanimously responded with, 'Good morning.'

Only after this greeting and the complete silence that followed were we allowed to sit down.

If there was no writing involved in the lessons, we had to keep our arms on our desk folded at a 90-degree angle. The right arm had to lay on top of the left arm. If one of us wanted to ask a question or to show the teacher that we knew an answer, we had to raise our right arm up. When raising the arm, both elbows had to touch the surface of the desk. If a teacher caught a pupil that didn't know an answer, they hit the pupil's nails with a ruler, pulled them by their ear or braids or forced them to stand in the front corner of the classroom.

In first grade, all Latvian children already had to take Russian language lessons. During those classes we mostly had to read poems and stories about Lenin and discuss his glorious achievements. That is how I learned what an outstanding human he was, an example to all of us. The poems taught us that we all had to strive for perfection. Lenin always scored the highest grades at school, which were fives. On the first day of school, I made a promise to my parents that I too would score only fives at school.

During the breaks, all the kids had to leave the classroom and walk in circles in the hallway. On one end of the hallway was a wall of fame with all the most outstanding pupils on our floor. I looked up to them. After first grade, my classmate Sonya's portrait was already up on this wall and I envied her. She had only fives.

At least, one teacher was present to supervise the breaks, making sure we all walked in pairs, in the same direction, and at exactly the right pace. That teacher also monitored whether we were having appropriate conversations. Once the supervising teacher corrected me.

'You are supposed to discuss the newly taught material with your classmate, just like the Russian children do it, instead of talking about non-study related things.'

Every pupil in our school had the same white school diaries with bilingual text on the cover that required filling in personal details, including the name of the school, grade, year and the name of the pupil. Everybody also had the same green notebooks for taking notes during class. My notebooks looked very elaborate and most of them even had portraits of our glorious leaders and other Soviet heroes like Lenin, Stalin and Gagarin[17].

We had heroes amongst the employees of my school, too. On the 2nd floor, there was a permanent display of the "employees of the month". Next to these portraits there were calligraphic posters listing all their glorious achievements. Sometimes after my classes, while waiting for my mother to pick me up, I lingered around the employees of the month boards to read about them. All of their achievements had to do with promoting communism through amateur activities with the Young Pioneers, such as amateur theatre, amateur ensembles and choirs and pioneer camps.

---

[17] This type of propaganda notebook was last printed in the '70s, which means that my parents got them from somebody who still had a stash of unused notebooks at home.

Hairy Story #3

In my class, there was a quiet boy named Emil. He often skipped school, had bad grades and so he had to repeat first grade several times. I had heard rumours that Emil came from a very poor family. He was much older than me. Teachers called him stupid and threatened him with staying a first grader until his beard started to grow. After such public shamings, Emil would disappear for days, and when he reappeared, he always avoided eye contact.

One day, after one of his long periods of absence, Emil showed up again at school. He seemed a bit dirty. My teacher suspected that Emil had lice as he kept on scratching his head. Not long after that she sent Emil home.

'Tell your mother that she should take better care of you.'

Embarrassed and humiliated, Emil left the classroom. At home, even though I knew my mother never wanted to hear anything about other children, I told her that Emil had lice.

The next morning my head was itchy. My mother took a close look at my hair and found lice.

'You're going to miss a few classes today,' she said as she urged me and my sisters into the bathroom, which was fortunately free at the time. We sat down on the edge of the bathtub waiting for my mother to open a bottle and pour a stinky liquid straight into our hair. She rubbed the lotion thoroughly until every hair on my head was moist. She gathered my hair on top of my head, twist ed it in a bundle and then pulled a plastic bag on my head, as if it was a hat. I thought we weren't allowed to put plastic bags on our head.

'Mum, what are you doing?' I asked.

'It's to prevent the lice from jumping away,' she answered.

My sisters went through the same treatment, after which we were sent to our room. We laughed at each other for looking so stupid. Waiting for half an hour with a plastic bag on my head was rather uncomfortable. My head was itchy and there was no way to scratch it properly through the plastic. My skull felt squeezed and my head was sweating. Finally, my mother called me back into the bathroom. I had to sit on my knees and bend my head over the edge of the bathtub. My mother combed my hair thoroughly, inspecting every dead louse that landed on the bottom of the tub. Then she searched my hair and pressed down with her nails at different spots on my head.

'Ouch, what are you doing, Mum?' I asked.

'I'm popping the nasty lice eggs so they won't hatch,' she answered.

There was a certain tone of satisfaction in her voice. After a successful massacre, my mother washed my hair, wrapped a towel around my head and called in my sisters for the exact same procedure.

Around noon, my mother finally brought me to school.

'Don't tell anybody about the lice.' She admonished me. 'We are a good family,' she said.

I arrived right on time for the lunch break and went straight to the canteen. The seat next to my friend was empty. Surprised to see me, she asked where I was in the morning.

'Oh, yeah, so I had lice and my mother put a plastic bag on my head. But don't worry, all the lice are dead, she double checked it,' I assured my friend.

'Your mother did what?' she asked in a loud voice.

'Quiet,' I whispered, 'I'm not supposed to tell anybody about it. I'm from a good family, you know.'

An Example of Good Behaviour

On Sunday evenings, I watched my mother unclip, wash and iron my collar and uniform sleeves. On Monday mornings, I buttoned them onto my dark blue dress. Compared to my other classmates, the wrinkly edge of my collar and sleeves was very narrow and simple-looking but at least they were always ironed and perfectly white. My classmate Emil's uniform sometimes appeared messy. If the teacher noticed that she walked up to him, grabbed him by his ear and commanded him to, 'Go home and don't come back until your clothes are washed and ironed.'

One time during our "Good Behaviour" class, the neatness of our uniforms was the topic of the day. When that lesson start ed, our teacher sat down on the ground instead of the chair behind her desk. The floor at the front part of the classroom was one step higher than the rest of the room but our eyes still had to be lowered to see her. She sat down on the edge of the little pedestal and put a book on her lap, creating a cosier atmosphere. In a sincere voice, she started reading aloud a story about a soldier who wanted to notify his commanding officer about an explosion. When the soldier ran into the officer's room, the officer looked at the soldier's uniform and asked him to leave the room immediately, look at himself in the mirror, fix his collar and only then come back. While the teacher was reading the story, I felt more and more confused. I couldn't grasp that the rule of maintaining a neat uniform remained a strict requirement even in a life-threatening situation. But from the tone of her voice I knew that she was presenting this story as a positive example.

In Good Behaviour classes, every story was followed by a discussion. Before the teacher closed the book, I sunk down into the chair of my desk as low as I could trying to make myself invisible. I looked in confusion at the sea of the enthusiastic raised hands and the sparkling eyes of my classmates, who all eagerly wanted to make a comment on the importance of the neat-looking uniform. I sympathised with the soldier who didn't care about his collar but I knew I would get into serious trouble if I said that.

Meet My Swimming Teacher

I remember the day my teacher announced that we were going to take swimming classes. The idea of swimming lessons was exciting and frightening at the same time. I had never been swimming in nature, nor had I visited the swimming pool. My most impressive full-body water-related experience was in the bathtub in Kommunalka, which is why I was sure I didn't know how to swim. My mother saw that I was worried and told me that all I had to do was move like a frog. Then she showed me the arm movement. I knew from my older sister that during swimming classes she learned to swim comfort ably on her back and she even liked it.

On the day of the swimming lesson, my classmates gathered around the swimming teacher. Her body was bulky, her shoulders were wide and strong, and the look in her eyes was intimidating. First, she showed us the correct movements on dry land, then we all had to repeat them. This part of the lesson counted as the warm-up after which we all went to the changing room to get into our swimsuits.

During our swimming lesson the entire pool was available just for my class. The swimming teacher held a wooden rod and yelled out commands of what we had to do. Her first order.

'Stand in a queue and one after another jump into the water.'

I was so frightened of the depth of the pool that I kept letting other pupils pass in front of me. Sonya, Ella and I lingered as the last ones at the edge of the pool, until eventually even they overcame their fear and jumped into the water. And there I was, the last one standing. The teacher saw me hesitate and screamed at me.

'Jump!'

But I didn't.

'Should I push you?' she asked.

I shook my head and clearly said, 'No.'

I trembled from fear and cold, barely standing on my legs, which were turning weaker and softer. To encourage myself, I started to count down and then I jumped into the water before a new wave of fear could kick in. I didn't expect feeling so disoriented under the surface of the water. I didn't know I had to take a deep breath before the jump and my nose and mouth had been open. I panicked under water, gasping for air, and my lungs filled with liquid. When I surfaced, I was coughing out water fighting my way towards my classmates who held onto the edge of the pool. Everybody was so intimidated by the teacher that nobody dared to laugh at me.

The next command was to cross the width of the pool. Again, we had to swim one by one. The teacher stood on the other side of the pool and stuck out her wooden rod for the kids who needed some extra help. Sonya, Ella and I were on the drowning end.

'You won't let go of the wood?' a frightened Ella asked.

'No, just hold on to it,' the teacher answered.

Cramped at the edge of the pool, I watched Ella and Sonya bravely cross. The swimming teacher commanded me to swim and my classmates were encouraging me. I stayed still. The teacher grabbed the wooden rod and walked around the pool in my direction. When she almost reached my side of the pool, in fear of getting beaten I let go of the wall and in a panic, I pushed my body towards the middle of the pool. I didn't know how to move my limbs and I was drowning in my own splashes. When I started to disappear under the surface, my classmate Egmond swam out and dragged me to the other side of the pool. Egmond was my saviour and my classmates were cheering for his bravery.

The third and last assignment was swimming the length of the pool. We were split into pairs to compete with each other. Those who reached the end of the pool were immediately graded and were then free to go to the changing room. I tried to swim but I never reached the other end of the pool. In tears, I swam to the metal stairs and climbed out. My teacher sent me to the changing room and graded my drowning at a three, the lowest sufficient grade for passing a subject at school.

Meet Mrs Bumblebee and Mrs Swan

Rhythmics was one of my favourite classes. In this class, children were taught to have a sense of rhythm through dance. Mrs Swan was our enthusiastic teacher. When the music was playing, she typically stood in the middle of the room, clapping her hands to the beat, shouting out to the children what movement they had to do. All the girls had to wear the same outfit. A black top with a red skirt. Boys wore a white t-shirt with black shorts that looked a lot like black underpants. Both boys and girls had special footwear called "cheshkas", which were made of thin leather and tied to the foot with a sewn-in rubber band. Cheshkas were so thin that they allowed for full flexibility of the toes.

The lesson always took place in the same room where we held school concerts, graduation events and the so-called "Line". During the "Line", the school director addressed several (sometimes even all) classes with a lecture intended to shame us by drawing attention to bad behaviour, sometimes even of just one pupil, which was presented to everybody as a bad example. The Line was a feature the entire time I went to school and it always served the same purpose of group guilt tripping.

During every Rhythmics lesson there was live piano music provided by an adorable lady named Mrs Bumblebee. Mrs Bumblebee was very old. She had long, curly, grey hair, a hawkish nose, a hunchback and she always wore long, floaty dresses. Mrs Bumblebee loved children so much that she continued working even though she seemed ancient. While Mrs Swan was explaining something to pupils, Mrs Bumblebee often fell asleep. She snored very loudly.

If the snoring became too distracting, Mrs Swan loudly clapped her hands and shouted, 'Mrs Bumblebee, Mrs Bumblebee, we need polka.'

Mrs Bumblebee could wake up and fall asleep in a second and at that same speed she could swap between melodies. She often played while sleeping and I admired her for that.

Grandpa Lenin Would Not Be Proud

One of my strongest memories from elementary school is the class excursion we took to a museum in Jurmala. I had just turned nine years old. We took a train, the same train that I always took with my parents when going to our dacha. We even got off at the same train station. To me it was strange to be at this familiar place as a visitor and to see it before the holiday season began. On the way to the museum, some children asked our teacher if they could check out the souvenir shop and the teacher agreed. At first, I waited outside of the shop with Ella and our teacher. One by one our classmates exited the shop showing off their plastic dolphin rings. After having waited until almost everyone was finished, Ella and I decided to enter the shop as well. My mother had given me some coins for the trip.

I was the last person in the queue, right behind Ella. When Ella bought her ring, she immediately went outside. Then she rushed back inside to tell me that everybody was gone. Ella was very worried. First, we waited for about fifteen minutes. I watched Ella become more and more anxious. I knew the environment so well that I was completely calm. Then I told her that our dacha was just around the corner and that it had a swing we could use while we waited. Eventually I convinced her to come with me. I ran to the swing and Ella sat down on the wooden stairs of our veranda. She was crying. I asked her if she wanted to see the beach but she refused to go any further. She was clearly not in the mood for sightseeing. She begged me to walk her back to the shop. We stood there for a good half an hour but nobody came looking for us. I suggested to Ella that we go back to Riga but she refused that too. I told her that I was done waiting and I was going to go back home. Then I walked by myself to the station, bought a train ticket and went home.

Later that evening some classmates phoned Kommunalka to ask what had happened. They said that the class teacher was sitting at the Mylicija (Soviet police) office, crying. When my parents came home, they were surprised to find me there. I didn't have the keys to our Kommunalka, but when I rang the doorbell, Sveta let me in. I told my parents what had happened and to my surprise they said that it was the teacher's fault, that she was supposed to count the children before moving on to the next location. The next day was the last day of the study year which was a big celebration where we received our grades. My teacher ignored me, and I saw that she graded my behaviour throughout all of elementary school at a 3, the lowest grade possible while still passing. It was my last grade earned in the Soviet grading system.

How I Learned About the
Properties of Bread and Aluminium

Soviet school cafeterias set a very low standard for becoming an aristocrat. If I had been picky about cutlery, like my aristocrat mother, I would have starved to death. All the cafeteria cutlery in the Soviet Union was made of aluminium. It was very soft and easy to deform. At school, there were always some boys that couldn't resist the temptation to bend the handles and prongs of the forks. I was incredibly annoyed if one of those was the only tool available for my lunch.

Other than that, food always made me happy. Even though I came from a so-called "big" family (a family with three or more children), and I got a free, state-funded two-course lunch at school, sometimes I still craved more. Then I, or one of my classmates, would patrol the canteen to check whether it was busy. After our canteen spy gave us the signal, we would sneak inside to stuff our pockets with slices of "black brick" bread. If we got unlucky, we were chased away by the kitchen staff. But there were also some kitchen ladies that had lots of compassion for hungry kids. If they had cooked too much soup, they might serve us an extra plate. Sometimes we stuffed our uniform pockets with bread even if we were not hungry. We did it just in case we felt hungry later that day. On many Monday mornings, when dressing up for school, I found hard, dried-out slices of bread in the pockets of my school uniform.

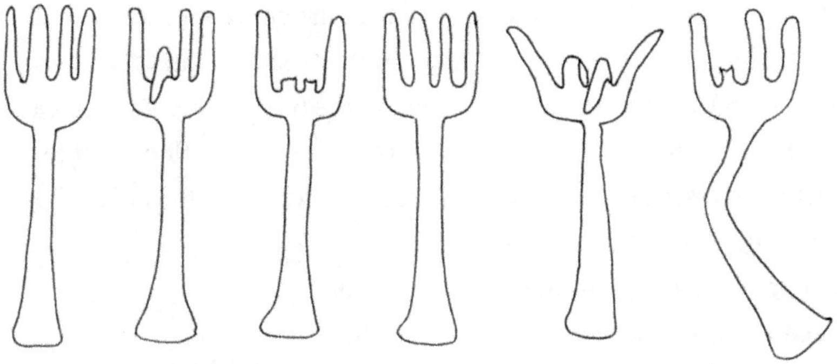

Tuo-Cha

There were about 1,500 pupils in my school spread throughout an L-shaped three-storey building. There were six toilets in the entire school. We called them "tuo-cha". The only teacher's toilet was on the first floor and the key for it had to be picked up from the receptionist. Next to the tiny teacher's toilet was a girl's toilet but for girls the most popular one was on the ground floor next to the sport hall. There was a serious reason for this preference; it was the only toilet open to pupils that could be locked with a hook.

The rest of the toilets were on the other end of the school, one on each floor. On the top floor was a boy's and a girl's toilet for the elementary school. One floor below was the girl's toilet for the primary and high school and on the first floor was the corresponding boy's toilet.

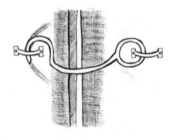

The boy's toilet was the smelliest corner of the school. The odour of urine was so imposing that if you happened to be on the first floor for the first time you would be able to locate the toilet immediately from afar. One time my curiosity got the better of me and I secretly entered the boy's toilet for an inspection. As with the girl's toilet there were two spaces. But in the boy's toilet, in the open space right at the entrance, opposite from the sinks, there was one big communal rectangular urinal on the ground which implied that during busy times several boys would have to stand around it at once while they peed. The edges of the urinal were made of tiles and the surface was covered by a metal sheet with holes. There was no way of flushing; the urine had to leak into the sewer by itself.

That explains the stink, I thought to myself. Next to the space with the urinal there was an area with regular toilet pots.

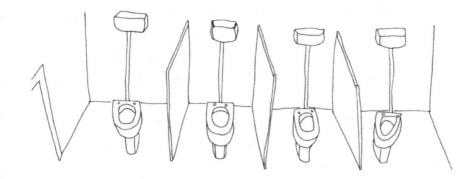

The toilet that I most commonly used was the one above that boy's toilet. In the girl's version, there were only sinks and mirrors on the wall where the boys had their urinal. There was no door to the second space and everybody could walk in freely. In both the boy's and girl's toilets, there were only small, narrow separation walls in between the toilet pots which were placed in a row. Everybody who had to queue for a spot often unwillingly ended up watching those who were on the toilet. The most convenient solution was to avoid the toilet completely by drinking as little as possible and when this method ultimately failed, to run across the entire building to check if the lockable toilet at the sport hall was open.

The older I grew the more uneasiness I started to experience as a result of the lack of privacy at school. I noticed more frequently the pattern of girls raising their hand during class and asking for permission to go to the restroom. Not all teachers were understanding and the comments "pee in your pants", "wait until the break", "we just had a break" and "drink less" were very common. When I started getting my periods, the lack of privacy hit me hard. There was one particularly memorable time when I went to the restroom during class and found myself struggling with a bloody mess. Suddenly two older girls came in and I felt caught. I was embarrassed to deal with personal hygiene of this sort in the plain sight of other people. The girls pointed at me, whispered something in each other's ears and laughed. To this day I cannot understand why they would be this mean when they also had to deal with their periods in the same way.

For several years after Latvia regained its status as an independent democratic republic, the toilets remained the same. The first opportunity for a change occurred in the spring of 1996 when a group of enthusiastic high school students organised the very first school elections. Several parties were formed and each of them hung promotional posters that listed various promises for improvement. Naturally, my vote went for the party that promised to install toilet doors. That party won the elections. After the elections, the school director was pressured to make plans for toilet improvement and eventually she made the announcement that the first modern toilets would be installed after the summer break.

In autumn that same year, I returned to school as a high school student and I was excited to check out the new toilets. To my great disappointment the first upgrade was made on the floor for the elementary school, to show off how modern our school was to the first-grader parents and the director warned that pupils from the higher grades were strictly forbidden to use those toilets. Though I never broke that rule, I did go to see how the new toilets looked. A whole new world unravelled in front of my eyes. There was a row of cabins with beautiful doors that could be locked, the new toilet pots where shiny and white, and on the wall of each toilet compartment hung a roll of beautiful, white, soft toilet paper.

It took another year or two for these improvements to hap pen in the rest of the school. After the renovation works, toilet paper was still a rare item, at least in the girl's toilet, but at least the smelly, old Soviet pots with their permanent rust lines were finally gone. The lack of privacy in earlier years had caused me to suffer from toilet trauma[18]. I definitely appreciated that I could finally lock the door behind me but I still tried to only visit the restroom when I was sure I could be all alone in the entire space. The new doors did not reach the ground or the ceiling and so I was annoyed if I entered the toilet and found girls in front of the mirror fixing their hair and make-up and gossiping about boys. I knew if I could hear them they could hear me.

---

[18] My female classmates from that time, many of whom I am still in touch with, admit having similar issues.

Part II

For Two Weeks, I Didn't Have a Name

When I was ten, my classmate told me that his little sibling was in his mother's belly.

'What nonsense,' I told him. 'If children grow in their mothers' bellies, I would remember being in my mother's belly.'

Irritated, I cut our conversation short. I wasn't buying this stupid story. Children were either brought into families by storks or found in cabbage fields (my father even said that annoying kids had been found in sour cabbage patches).

In reality, just like any other child in Soviet Riga, I was born in the birthing hospital. It was 1983 and to the best of my memory, it was a Monday morning. That day the first blossoms appeared on the trees. I was one week overdue and yet my mother had still planned to go to the movies that day. On every birthday, I had to hear my mother talk about the film screening she missed. She also reminded me how ugly I was when I was born. According to her, I had rough and slightly yellow skin. She didn't want to touch me until I started looking less gross.

My mother told me that for the first two weeks of my life I didn't have a name. She also said that my father, in disappointment at not getting a son, didn't have any name options and my mother took her time to think. She loved reading books. If I can trust her stories, in her early youth she was so often sick that out of boredom she learned to read, so that by the age of four she had read the epic Greek poems of *The Iliad* and *The Odyssey*. My mother considered naming me Penelope, after the wife of Odysseus. But when she saw me eagerly screaming for milk, she decided that this name didn't quite suit me.

After scratching Penelope off the name options list, my mother thought of another name. At work, she sometimes joined illegal screenings of western films. Once when they watched an Italian movie (unfortunately I don't know the title), she noticed a nice name and she really liked the sound of it. That name did not exist in the Soviet Union but my mother didn't find it important to give me a name that was on the calendar[19]. My name had to sound nice, had to be easy to pronounce and preferably wouldn't contain language-specific letters. She had a feeling that one day I would become internationally famous and she gave me a name that everybody would be able to pronounce when it appeared on large posters.

---

[19] In many Eastern European countries, it was and still is a custom to celebrate "Name's days". There is a list of names for each day on the calendar. A person's Name's day is celebrated as much as their birthday, with the one key difference that people get invited to birthdays, while on a Name's day, anybody is allowed to show up to congratulate the person. On the day a person's name appears on the calendar, their house and their table have to be prepared for a party.

How I Met My Younger Sister

In my parents' room, perched on the glass door of the cupboard, was a black-and-white photograph. My father took it when my mother had just returned home from the birthing hospital holding my baby sister wrapped in a blanket. On one side of my mother stood my older sister, happily smiling and looking with curiosity at the baby, and on the other side I stood, looking straight into the camera with an expression somewhere between anger, jealousy and fear and with a little accent of a worry in my eyebrow.

For years, I had difficulty accepting that the tiny bits of parental attention that we could get all went to my little sister. Because of this, I often tried to convince my little sister that she didn't belong in our family and that she was adopted.

Meet My Older Sister

Once upon a time my older sister drew a beautiful princess on the wall in our room with a green wax crayon. The princess had on a pretty dress and wore a crown on her head. I liked her drawing so much that I decided to make my own mural drawing, too. I drew a sailboat. These two drawings said a lot about our differences; she was sophisticated and I was simple. I always looked up to my older sister. She had shiny golden hair, blue eyes and a perfect smile.
'What an Angel,' people always exclaimed.

Everything she touched looked pretty and well-made. She always came up with creative ideas and fun games, she loved to dance, to draw and to style our hair. When she touched my hair, I got goose bumps, the nice ones.

Around the corner from our house was the Riga Fashion House. There was a garbage container near the fence that surrounded it. Sometimes we found little pieces of leftover fabric laying on the ground next to the bin. If the gate was open, we snuck inside to collect these exotic-looking pieces. I admired their beautiful prints and the interesting textures that were created by the woven, shiny threads. These leftovers inspired my older sister to make glamorous clothes for our dolls and eventually we organised a doll fashion show.

When I was about five years old, my older sister started attending afternoon ballet classes. There she learned the basic ballet positions. She could graciously hold her back straight, suck in her belly and butt and set her arms and fingers in an elegant curve above her head, all while holding a glowing smile. In my eyes, my sister was the perfect candidate for the professional ballet school.

My sister taught the ballet postures to me and my little sister, and I thought that if I practiced them then one day, I would also be able to join the ballet class. One afternoon, when we went to pick her up, it was audition day for new girls and I joined in. The lady teaching the ballet class spoke only Russian and nearly all the little girls were Russian. We all had to repeat the movements that the teacher made. I did my best but got the feeling that I was not going to be selected.

Without finishing my audition I ran to my mother. Then my mother told me that Russian girls are much more suitable for ballet because of their finer skeleton and lighter bones.

'Your older sister got luckier with her bone structure. You are heavily built, like a typical Latvian girl,' she said with regret.

In first grade, I was jealous but also proud of my older sister. She was two grades above me and she wore a red "Little Octobrists star"[20] pinned to her chest. This star was an award that was handed out to all children when they reached second grade. My sister told me that in fifth grade she was going to become a Young Pioneer. She said that Young Pioneers had to wear a red scarf around their neck, they learned to march and on Lenin's birthday they had to bring flowers to his monument. The Soviet Union fell apart right before I could become Little Octobrist. My older sister never became a Young Pioneer. Instead, she followed my mother's dream and at the age of ten she got admitted into the professional ballet school. From then on, my entire family was on a diet in forced solidarity. My sister's school schedule changed from five working days to six. She always left early in the morning and returned home late in the evening. I saw her very little and soon I knew almost nothing about her life. On Saturdays, my older sister left for school before my mother cooked Hercules. When she came back in the afternoon, upon her arrival, a cold and stiff Hercules was awaiting her. She too was disgusted by the porridge but she could escape with just one spoonful and earn a tasty curd snack.

My older sister and I shared a bunkbed. My mother strongly believed that the bed would collapse under my weight if I was on top so she told my light-boned older sister to take the top bunk. There she kept all her most valuable belongings. On Sundays, she sat in bed binding her bloody toes and darning the holes in her ballet shoes. Sometimes her toes hurt so much that I could hear her quietly sob. On those days, she preferred to pick a fight so that she could avoid

---

[20] The code of the Little Octobrists:

* Little Octobrists are future Young Pioneers.
* Little Octobrists are studious, they study well, they love school and they respect their elders.
* Little Octobrists are honest and truthful.
* Little Octobrists are friendly, they read and they draw, they play and they sing and they live happily. Only those who love to work can earn the title of Little Octobrist.

talking to us. I already saw her so little that this created an even greater distance between us and made me bond more with my little sis ter. One morning, when I woke up, I slowly opened my eyes and saw something strange on the elbow joint of my arm; a sharp sewing needle had fallen and its tip was stuck in my skin. Then I remembered that on the previous day my sister had been looking for a lost needle.

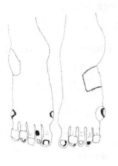 

In the ballet school, my older sister had to wear an exclusively white outfit. White top, white tights, ballet shoes and a white skirt. Her hair had to be wrapped in a perfect bun and any loose hair had to be pinned flat. When school concerts were approaching, she would bring home classic short and long tutu dresses. She let me and my little sister try them on. I was taller than her and could barely fit in them but trying on these dresses made me feel very elegant and pretty, like a princess. I loved their texture, the fine details of the stitches and the wrinkled tulle fabric. I was surprised when I saw these dresses up close – these elegant garments that looked on the stage as if they were made of soft, fluffy feathers, were actually made of a rough and sharp material.

I was overwhelmingly proud when my older sister landed a role in the National Theatre, playing a little bird in the play *Christmas Star*. I watched the show so many times that I knew it by heart. During the rehearsal period my sister bonded with an actor and he gave her an amazing present, an actor's makeup set. In the ballet school, she had make-up classes and now she was the one with the most elaborate make-up set at school. Me and my younger sister loved to be her models and she liked to practise on us. In the summer, when we were at our dacha and our parents were not home, my older sister would give us special make-up. She painted my nose red and made my eyes look swollen like an alcoholic and my little sister got a layer of makeup that made her look like she got a black eye in a fight. Once the make-up was done I grabbed an empty beer bottle and went on a drunk walk in the garden. When other parents saw us looking like this, they got so furious that they took their kids inside. I guess my sister's makeup skills were so good that we soiled our image as a good family.

At the ballet school, my sister became best friends with a girl named Lynn. The two girls were inseparable but my mother disliked their friendship. She said that Lynn was bad influence because she was vegetarian, ate soy products and listened to Michael Jackson. According to my mother, people had to eat real meat rather than strange surrogates. As she was forever an ABBA and The Beatles fan, Michael Jackson wasn't her cup of tea. In secret, we listened to his music anyway, and we even sang along, pronouncing the lyrics the way we heard them. As I went to a French school I started learning English later.

On weekdays, Lynn stayed in the ballet boarding school and my mother hated that my sister begged to also be sent to the boarding school. But my sister was simply exhausted from having to commute six days a week.

'Only children who are not loved by their parents are placed in an institution like the boarding school,' said my mother.

As my sister repeatedly brought up the boarding school in their conversations, I was scared that one day she would manage to convince my parents to enrol her and then I would never see her again.

I had seen Lynn's mother a few times in the audience at the ballet school concerts. She appeared to take care of herself well and she was much more modern than my parents. Her appearance made me curious and I asked my older sister some questions. She explained that Lynn's mother was doing charity work and had some connections with the western world. It is thanks to her that my older sister sometimes brought home big bags filled with second-hand clothes from the west. When my sister unpacked the bags, my mother always looked through the clothes before anything was handed out to me and my little sister. If there were items that my mother liked and could fit into she confiscated them.

On days when my sister came home from school later than expected, my mother boiled in anger, hissing about surrogates and the shrieking music. She looked for ways to get us to tell on my older sister. Once, when I had an argument with my older sister, I used some remarks that I heard my mother make and my sister screamed at me that she could trust her friends more than her own sisters. I was hurt and embarrassed to hear those words. I knew her statement was true. We were trapped in a family situation where we were punished for any minor thing and so we often chose to tell on each other just to stay out of trouble with our parents. For that I hated myself and the conditions in which I grew up.

Meet Our Fourth Sister

My mother grew up as a single child; she knew all about feeling lonely. In addition to promoting the good cause of growing the population, she also thought that three children would always have some company for each other. But even though I grew up with two sisters, I still sometimes felt lonely.

Once my sisters and I fantasised about how great it would be if we had another sister. And that's when my older sister came up with an idea; if our parents aren't going to do it, we could make a fourth sister ourselves. One of her toys was a stuffed monkey. It was so big that its head was just a tiny bit smaller than ours. We dressed the monkey in a dress that didn't fit any of us anymore and we extended its legs with pantyhose that we stuffed with our clothing. Then we built a castle for the fourth sister out of our little dining table, chairs and blankets. We treated her like a princess.

Family Photo Album

I don't have any photographs of myself as a baby. My mother didn't like photographs[21].

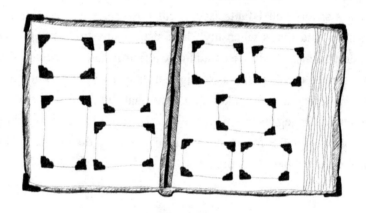

---

[21] I always found it very contradictory that both my parents were involved in the film and photography industry but hadn't made a family photo album. When my father was in a good mood, he took a few photos of me and my sisters in our home, but that was an exception. I was always jealous to see the photographs of my classmates. When I confronted my mother about it, she said she saw no use in photographs – instead, she preferred to observe and memorise the things she liked. I could only conclude that in her eyes, my growing up concerned her more than me. When I pointed that out, she had no appropriate counter-argument. I just had to accept things as she had decided them to be, for in my family the oldest one was always right.

Director Exploded and All the Dolls
Got Poisoned

In April of 1986, one day after I turned three, a catastrophic nuclear accident occurred in Chernobyl. I was too young to understand what this disaster meant and for many years I lived with my own misinterpretation of the event. Considering the extent of the impact of the Chernobyl disaster the entirety of occupied Latvia counted as relatively close to the zone of radiation. My mother didn't allow us to stand in direct sunlight. She had this inner sense when the radiation in our area was too high and her suspicions were always confirmed by the news on the radio.

Months after the Chernobyl accident, radio journalists reported on giant mushrooms that were seen in the forest. They warned people not to eat them. I could never understand what exactly people like about these things that are covered with slime, that smell like earth and become even smellier when cooked. Now that I knew that the mushrooms in our area were radioactive, I was relieved that I never craved something that could potentially kill me. In my world, mushrooms were not to be trusted. Like my father, I couldn't digest mushrooms but at the same time I hoped to spot a giant one in the woods.

After the nuclear tragedy, my parents attended the Film Symposium which featured documentaries about Chernobyl. As true "kinoshniki" (a Russian slang word that people professionally involved in the film industry called each other, regardless of whether they spoke Latvian or Russian), my parents didn't want to miss this event and they wanted to see as many documentaries as possible. For most of the films, they took turns, but there was one documentary that neither of my parents wanted to miss, so they took us along to the screening. I remember sitting on the right side of my father with my little sister right next to me. On the screen, I saw a room filled with empty beds and abandoned dolls.

'What is this?' I whispered in my father's ear.

'It's a kindergarten,' he whispered back.

These hostile images made no sense to me so I asked him what happened.

My father whispered back, 'Director exploded and all the dolls got poisoned.'

For years, I was very confused about this exploding director but I passed on the story to my sisters and friends. A few years later, when Chernobyl came up in a conversation with my friends, very wisely and with confidence I told the other kids that it was all because of a director who exploded. My older sister laughed at me and said that it was not a director but an exploding reactor.

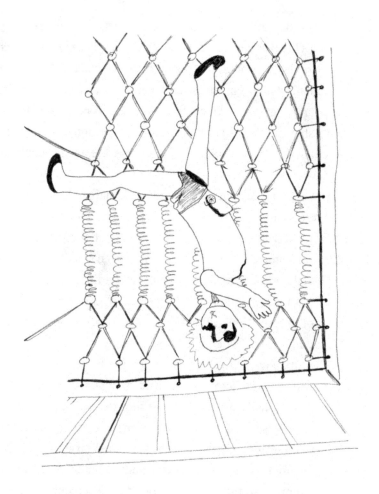

My African Doll

I was about four years old when a big earthquake hit Turkey. My mother rushed into our room holding a pair of jeans in her hands. Frantically, she started opening cupboards, pulling out drawers and ripping out clothes I didn't even know we had.

'There are people here that have come to collect things for the earthquake victims in Turkey. Pick a toy that you want to give to a child that has lost everything.'

Without a shadow of a doubt, I gave away my favourite[22] toy, an African doll. It was a dark brown plastic doll that had two simple rings around her neck as necklaces and it wore a green skirt that my older sister had made for her.

---

[22] When I was a teenager, I told my mother that on that day I had given away my favourite doll, and as a kid I really missed it. Donating to the earthquake victims taught me the importance of being empathic. My mother had been feeling guilty about me giving away my favourite toy, and when I was in my early twenties, she gave me another African doll to relieve her guilt.

Do You Want to See Moscow?

My father once told me about a nasty trick that some kids like to pull in the winter. First, they ask a younger kid, 'Do you want to see Moscow?' Moscow was known to be an amazing city as it was the capital of the Soviet Union. If the younger kid said "yes", then the older kid told them to touch their tongue to the bars of the metallic jungle gyms on the playground. My father told me that when it's freezing the bare moist skin of their tongue immediately freezes to the metal, so that the victim's tongue becomes stuck to the pole. And then the only way for them to disconnect is to use force and to lose a piece of the skin. After hearing about this disturbing joke, I had nightmares about bloody tongues and agonising pain. When I was on the playground, I feared finding a patch of tongue skin lying on the ground.

I Once Saw Moscow

Every cameraman from Riga Film Studio was supposed to personally bring their filmed material to the lab in Moscow to verify its content. This is why my father was frequently away. If he got lucky with his schedule and had an extra day, he always tried to escape into the streets and "sniff the world" in the shops. One could find everything in Moscow's stores, including products from the west.

One winter, when I was four, my father took me to Moscow on one of his work trips. I was excited about the opportunity and I was relieved I didn't have to lick any metal to see the notorious city. It was also my first experience flying and my strongest memory from it was the cigarette smell and the ashtray in the armrest of my airplane seat. To help pass time during the flight, my father gave me a cardboard clipboard with a sheet of paper and a pen. Drawing kept me busy.

When we arrived in Moscow, the sky was black. The city was like nothing I had ever seen before. It was very alive; the streets were filled with driving cars and many buildings were lit with big letters.

The next day it was very cold. My father and I were standing on a square.
'This is the Red Square,' he said.
I was confused. There was no red to be seen. Everything was covered with a layer of perfectly white snow. My father pointed at a building with beautiful colourful fairy-tale like rooftops.

'This is the Kremlin.'

'And right there is Lenin's Mausoleum.'

'What is a Mausoleum?' I asked.

He explained that when Grandpa Lenin died, he didn't get buried but was instead placed in the Mausoleum.

'Look at those queuing people, they have come here to see Grandpa Lenin's dead body.'

'Why would anybody want to see my grandpa dead?' I asked, confused.

I hadn't been to a funeral before but the idea of keeping a dead body above the ground on display for everybody felt really bizarre.

'He is not your grandpa; it's just what communists usually say. And for some people Lenin is a hero,' he answered. 'But not for us.'

Catching a Squirrel

On one boring winter evening, I was playing inside with my sisters. We were jumping and doing self-invented acrobatics. I came up with a new trick and decided to demonstrate it. I stepped on a couch and leaned backwards against the edge of my sister's baby bed, planning to land on my hands in a bridge posture. Something went wrong and the next thing I remember was crying from pain and my older sister running to my father. My right arm was shaking and I had no control over my fingers.

When my father rushed in, he looked at my arm and said, 'You again.'

From the tone of his voice, I knew I was in trouble.

My father helped me put on my winter coat and carried me outside in his arms. Both my sisters were galloping next to him through the dark streets of Old Riga. We were rushing to the doctor's office. We would be able to see the doctor without waiting in line. There were five nice toys on the shelf behind his desk. He asked me which toy I liked the most. With my left hand, I pointed at the squirrel. He took the squirrel and held it in front of me.

'Grab it with your right hand,' he said.

I tried as hard as I could but I had no control over my arm. It was just helplessly shaking. The doctor brought the squirrel closer to my hand and asked me to try again. I tried to move my arm towards the toy and I managed to grab it.

I suddenly dropped the squirrel and my arm started shaking again. The doctor said that we were going to try to catch the squirrel once more. My arm kept on shaking but the reward was too good to give up. I tried and I tried and then I finally managed. This time I felt my arm click back into place at the elbow joint. The doctor let me play with the squirrel for a bit. My sisters asked me if I would share the toy with them but I was too greedy.

I earned my trophy and had no intention of sharing it with anybody.

The fun of my victory was ruined when the doctor exclaimed "fixed". He pulled the squirrel out of my hands and wished us good night.

Can't You See I'm a Squirrel?

In my early youth, washing machines were not available in every household; instead, ekonomkas washed piles of dirty diapers and laundry by hand. That is probably the reason my mother already started to potty-train us at five months old. My family had a little, dark brown washing machine with the lovely name Malutka, which meant "Tiny". Sadly, Malutka, apart from looking cute, was more of a disaster than a help. It ripped everything it washed and damaged almost all our clothes beyond repair. As we were too poor to afford new clothing, we wore whatever Malutka left behind, and from then on, we washed our clothes by hand.

On the street, nobody stood out. Adults wore clothes in boring colours and school kids wore uniforms. Men and women had big puffy hair which was widely popular in the '80s. Riga Fashion House and Ogre Knitwear were the main local producers of clothes. They produced a certain number of new designs and those were the only designs available in the store. That resulted in people wearing the exact same clothes.

Women wore blouses made of almost completely see-through materials which meant their undergarments were clearly visible. I was too tempted to stare at all the wrong places, studying the lace on bras. Women also wore clothing with large shoulder pads that made them look more masculine. I didn't understand why women wanted to pretend to have wide shoulders but I also didn't spend too much time trying to figure that out. I was obsessed with the spongy softness of the shoulder pads. I loved to poke them. I put my fingers mostly on my mother's shoulders but sometimes I got exceptionally lucky when taking a ride in an overcrowded trolley-bus; strangers were often kind enough to squeeze a bit tighter together to free up a little space on the seat for me, and if that happened, then I leaned towards them and poked their shoulder pads. All they could do then was giggle.

Women who knew how to operate a sewing machine used clothing pattern cut-outs from Riga Fashion magazine. They had the chance to stand out from the crowd with an outfit that wasn't factory-made. These women were able to look different, at least until someone else walked down the street in clothes made from the same fabric. The ultimate skill for creating a unique look was to rework an old garment into a completely new design. My mother had no sewing skills. She only knew how to attach a button, patch a little hole or fix the coat pocket that I ripped again and again when I held onto it.

One winter my kindergarten teachers organised a concert where children had to dress up like forest animals. My mother spent hours making a costume for me. When she called me into her room to see her work, I was excited. In her hands, she held a dark brown, thick cotton object in the shape of a cane. She had used one side of a pair of knitted pantyhose and filled it up with old pieces of cloth.

'This is the tail for your squirrel costume,' she proudly announced.

After seeing the result, I didn't want to go up on stage anymore. My mother was furious about my ungrateful reaction. She had wasted her time and now I had to wear this custom-made costume. I felt even more insecure when I saw beautiful fluffy, furry tails on other kids. Embarrassed, I walked along the walls, trying to disappear from view. All the kids were comparing their costumes. When they saw me, they asked why I had a cane attached to my back. With tears in my eyes, I defended my mother's efforts.

'It's a tail. Can't you see I'm a squirrel?' This was my mother's first and last attempt at making a custom-made costume.

Born in a Queue, Raised in a Queue

When I was growing up, there was an ongoing deficit of everything. The state-maintained control over sales by handing out vouchers that allowed common people to queue in order to buy a certain amount of a specific product, such as alcohol, cigarettes, cleaning items and meat products. These vouchers were allocated per person, even if it was a newborn. The vouchers were distributed once a month and they were valid for a very short time. When shops received a new allotment of a product, ekonomkas all notified each other. There was no doubt about one thing; if you saw a queue, you had to queue.

Information travelled from mouth to ear very quickly and in no time long queues formed in front of stores. Passers-by asked the queuing people what they were queuing for and then they also joined the queue. When queuing, it was important to make friends with the person standing in front of and behind you, as you were dependent on their willingness to hold your spot in the queue in case you had to briefly leave. Sometimes my mother rushed home to get some money or to the kindergarten to pick me up. She then quickly got me ready and we hurried back to the queue. Queuing took hours. This is why Latvians adapted the lyrics of a Latvian folk song *Born singing, raised singing, spent my life singing* to *Born in a queue, raised in a queue, spent my life in a queue.*

Getting basic food products was a big struggle, even with state vouchers. My mother sometimes traded her White Death vouchers to a friend to get extra vouchers for flour or cheese in return. My mother's friend had relatives living in the countryside and they could use the extra sugar for making jam from fruits and berries in their garden. In our household, we hardly used any sugar and not using a voucher would be a waste.

Incidental queuers had to be lucky to have the right voucher with them and enough money in their wallet to buy what they needed, but they also had to hope that by the time they finished queuing there would still be something left on the shop shelves. Those who bought a lot were booed by others.

'Leave something to the rest of us!'

'But I have five children to feed.'

Or 'I'm buying it for my handicapped neighbour!' the person would exclaim in their own defence.

Zakroma Rodini

Once I entered a shop with my mother and we found two bored employees standing behind the counter with nothing to do. This was such a typical sight in the Soviet Union that there was even a saying "they pretend to pay us, we pretend to work". Along the walls of the shop there were shelves, on which were stacked row after row of the same product, green blocks of soap. My mother asked the employees if they knew when the product that she was looking for would be delivered but they didn't know. We didn't need soap and we left empty-handed.

My mother would also buy things that we didn't need. She said she bought it for "Zakroma rodini", which means "the garden of the homeland", an idiom that stands for the idea of collecting things for the future but never seeing them again. Sometimes she came home with the expression on her face of a successful hunter and she revealed the extra tableware set that she bought for when one of us would get married, or the oversized clothing she bought "for when you will grow taller, when you'll be older".

When I grew out of my clothes, she dove into our Zakroma rodini.

'It has to be somewhere,' she would say while digging in boxes, bags and suitcases, unwrapping an uncountable amount of textile items.

If there was no well-fitting or even oversized clothing in our Zakroma rodini, she said I had to eat less to be able to fit in the clothes I was wearing.

Once when my shoes got too tight she excavated a black leather pair from our Zakroma rodini. The shoes turned out to be two sizes too big. My mother had bought them in a period when I was growing fast and imagined that this would be my eventual foot size. When I walked in my new oversized shoes, my feet slid around and the only way to prevent the sliding was by curling up my toes.

Everything my parents paid for; they saw as an investment for life. My mother was convinced that the clothes we were wearing would eventually even be passed on to our own children. In my youth, she had stacked up so much stuff

129

that she couldn't remember what she had bought, and we ended up not only not using what we had, but even missing basic items.

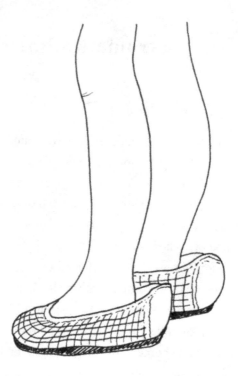

Another Soviet Luxury

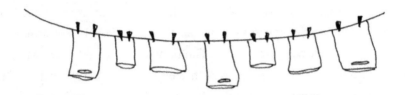

There wasn't much plastic in my childhood. Most toys were made of wood, metal and rubber. Plastic packaging also hardly existed. Nothing was thrown away and everything was reused until it fell apart.

We had a plastic case with a handle to carry eggs and we brought our own jars to the market to buy fresh cream and berries. If we bought dairy products in the shop, they came in glass bottles that were washed and sterilised at a recycling point.

No matter how fashionable people looked everybody carried reusable cotton or nylon bags and nets. When the first disposable plastic bags appeared in the Soviet Union, people handled them with great care as if they were a show-off luxury item from the west (or in the case of my family, as a lice-catcher). The plastic bags were washed and rinsed and then hung up on a clothing line for a public display. Once the sun and wind dried them, they could be reused over and over until the see-through bags turned opaque and the colourful prints on the white bags wore off and turned pale. While a plastic bag with a big print was a perfect handbag, a bag with a hole was a great loss. Even a damaged bag wasn't discarded, however – it was only downgraded to its new function, that of a wrapper.

The Privilege of Meeting Aunt Klara

My friends at school always had such nice stories to share about their grandmothers, grandfathers, uncles, aunts and even godfathers and godmothers that I listened to them with great envy. The only story I could share was about Aunty Klara, whom I had never met. In my early youth, I frequently suffered from middle ear infections. I remember having unbearable pain but my parents never gave me painkillers or antibiotics. My mother said that my body had to do all the work to strengthen itself. The only medicine that we used in our family to provide an extra boost to our bodies was ascorbic acid, which was highly concentrated vitamin C. In very severe cases, my mother put a compress on my ear, and wound it around my head with a red and white polka-dot scarf. To me this scarf was like a caring hug[23].

In our Kommunalka, the walls were made of thick stone but in the silence of the night any sound still came through easily, as if somebody amplified it. Our bedroom shared one wall with the communal bathroom, and when our neighbours were filling up the bathtub, I could hear the loud high-pitched peep from the worn-out hot water tap. When I was sick, the nights felt lonely and long

---

[23] To this day, I find a red fabric with white dots very soothing.

and I struggled to find a distraction from the pain. While my sisters were sleeping, I sat up in bed and silently cried until the peep from the tap stopped and in that silence I finally cried myself to sleep.

Usually, my infected ear episodes caused a temporary decline in my hearing. That's when my father would make an appointment with the "ear doctor" in a place called "the polyclinic". It was in a big, beautiful building that smelled strongly of drugs. The floor was covered with dark green tiles and at the entrance of the polyclinic was a pharmacy. Behind the desk stood a person in a white coat. I looked with great fascination at the shelves filled with brown bottles in various sizes. These bottles contained powders, pills and liquids.

When visiting the doctor, we first walked through the pharmacy, then continued down a narrow corridor passing by doors with frosted windows. I could hear voices behind the doors and I could see the moving silhouettes of people. At the end of the corridor, we reached the staircase and went up the stairs. Then we walked through another corridor until we reached a white door. My father knocked at the door and a tall man opened it for us. I saw a tiny room in front of me. The man had short grey hair and light blue eyes. He made eye contact with me. His name was Dr Drillmaster.

I was convinced he was called that because he was going to drill in my ear and that was a very frightening thought. Dr Drillmaster wore a metallic headband with a round mirrored disk attached to it. In the middle of that disk, there was a hole. He used this special headband as a tool for checking my ears. Even though Dr Drillmaster was always very gentle and patient with me, I was scared of these visits, just as others would be afraid to see the dentist. During these check-ups all I could think of was running away and he always had to order me to sit still. He explained that any wrong movement could cause permanent damage to my ear. The doctor inserted a metallic cone into my ear and slightly pulled on the soft part of my ear to have a better look. I could feel the warmth of the lightbulb. His eye looked huge in the mirror disk. Through the metallic cone he then inserted a hook in my hearing canal. It was both scary and painful. With the hook, he fished out excess earwax.

After this followed another unpleasant procedure, "the rinsing". Dr Drillmaster first placed an unusually shaped enamel dish on my shoulder, one that curved perfectly around my neck. Then he filled an intimidatingly large syringe with warm water and shot the water into my ear. I could see muddy-looking water flow into the enamel dish.

'It's the excess earwax that had clogged your hearing canal,' he explained.

When the water leaked out of my ear suddenly, I could hear again and everything sounded very clear and so loud that I wanted to cover my ears. Once when the doctor was rinsing my ear all the water came out clean. Surprised, he removed the syringe to have another look in my ear. Then we both noticed a big blob of ear wax stuck on the needle of the syringe.

'Do you have a cactus at home?' he asked.

'Yes, I have one,' I said.

With a piece of cotton, he removed the ear wax from the needle and told me to put it in the earth of the cactus pot.

'Ear wax is a great fertiliser.'

At the end of every appointment with doctor Dr Drillmaster, he asked me to repeat the same phrase several times – "Aunty Klara, Aunty Klara, Aunty Klara". While I was doing that, he picked up a little brown rubber balloon and squeezed it right at the moment when I said Aunty Klara – the sudden gust of pressurised air caused a nasty sensation in my nose and ear. It didn't take me long to figure out his trick and that was the end of my voluntary cooperation. I stopped responding and pretended I had turned transparent. In a calm and patient way, Dr Drillmaster tried to convince me to call for aunty Klara just one last time. When I saw my father's threatening stare out of the corner of my eye and I heard his sharp inhalation, I knew there would be consequences, and so out of fear I said "Aunty" at a normal speed and rushed through "Klara" so fast that the doctor missed his moment.

'Good girl, now say it slower,' he said.

I had no choice.

Somewhere around the beginning of the '90s my father came up with a reward if I was cooperative. After each visit to the doctor, he took me to the newspaper kiosk, where he allowed me to choose between Turbo and Donald Duck chewing gum – a product that was still rare and luxurious and for which for sure there was no money in my family budget. If my father bought me chewing gum, I swore to him that I would keep it a secret from my sisters and my mother. This reward made me feel like I was privileged to have ear pain.

The white blocks of chewing gum tasted plain, like sugar. Their real value wasn't in their flavour; kids bought chewing gum to collect the double wrapping. The inner wrapping had an image of a sports car or a tiny comic about Donald Duck. These pictures were called "fantiki" and kids traded them. The trading of fantiki happened within a game of fantiki. Those who wanted to play fantiki laid their collection down in one large stack. Then all players had to hit the stack with their palm in such a way that fantiki flew up in the air and got flipped around. The fantiki that got flipped around were the ones that the players could take for themselves. I wasn't very good at this game but watching others play it was exciting.

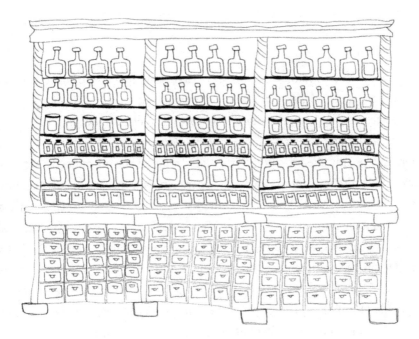

I Was Determined to Become
an Opera Singer

From my earliest childhood memories, music was my driving force. Through music I expressed my passion and emotions and in music I found a safe place where I belonged. When growing up, we rarely watched television. In our room, there was a radio on which we mostly listened to bedtime stories. In the daytime, I listened to opera. The presenter of the radio programme introduced opera artists by saying "With many merits awarded, opera singer xyz…" which was followed by a short story about their achievements. I loved hearing music and I was determined to become an opera singer. There were nights where my sisters asked me to sing a lullaby, which I gladly did, until I sang even myself to sleep. I was so fixated on becoming an opera singer that I didn't leave my mother alone until my parents signed me up for a vocal ensemble called The Sunshines.

One day my father brought me to the State Electrotechnical Factory Culture Palace. We got out at the trolleybus stop right in front of the palace and we saw a row of frames that proudly presented large portraits of the employees of the month. In the palace, my father introduced me to the couple that founded The Sunshines. We met in a little concert hall some time before the actual rehearsal. The couple was very friendly and smiley, especially the man. They asked me to sing a few songs – I sang my heart out. They admitted me to the ensemble that same day and I had my first rehearsal. I immediately loved it. I was about three and a half years old and I remained a member of this ensemble for about four years. This is where I learned to do vocal warm-ups and I filled my repertoire with many new songs. We had to perform in concert halls and on television so often that the stage quickly became my second home. I could sing very well and I sang at least one solo song at every con cert. Our repertoire was only in Latvian.

I must have been about five or six years old when I went with The Sunshines on a bus trip to Klaipeda in Lithuania. It was my first trip abroad without my parents and I was put under the supervision of two older girls in the group.

In Klaipeda, we stayed one night in a hotel. Along with the keys to the room we also received a coupon for a meal in the restaurant. In the evening, we all went for dinner. It was a buffet with portions pre-served on plates. The prices were not mentioned anywhere. We walked around the restaurant, picked what we wanted to eat and put it on the tray. Then we had to pass by the lady at the check-out. She meticulously noted all the contents on the tray. A boy from our ensemble, one who had recently joined and who was also there without his parents, was queuing at the check-out right in front of me. After the check-out, lady had noted down everything that the boy had chosen, she gave him a bag of yellow, green and red candies. *How odd,* I thought. When it was my turn at the check-out, I also got a bag of candies. One of the mothers that was standing behind me asked the lady in Russian[24] why the candies were handed out. The check-out lady explained that the coupon was of a certain value and those who selected food under that value got the rest compensated in candies. I noticed a spark of joy in the boy's eyes as he overheard the conversation.

In the hotel, I shared a room with the two older girls who were supervising me. After dinner, the vocal coach told me to go to bed. I immediately walked to the room, brushed my teeth, undressed and went to sleep. I fell asleep before the older girls arrived. I was in a deep sleep when I was woken up by the two girls. They were already dressed. They were shaking me, saying that I was late for the rehearsal, and that I had to hurry up. I was so embarrassed about being late that I quickly pulled my clothes on and rushed into the corridor. I bumped straight into my vocal coach and with a smile said, 'Good morning.' She asked me where I was going, and I said, 'To the rehearsal.' She got very upset and told me that she was going to complain to my parents about my misbehaviour. I was confused. When I walked back into my hotel room, the two older girls couldn't stop laughing. They opened the curtain to show me the night sky. Only then did I realise that the two girls had tricked me. I went to bed hiding my tears. I had a big lump in my throat and I was scared of the punishment that awaited me back home.

---

[24] In the Soviet Union, Russian was the main language of communication, and it was always used if people of different nationalities from the Soviet Union were having a conversation.

The next morning we had only a short window of time to eat our breakfast as we had to rush to rehearsal afterwards. When I picked up my tray in the restaurant, the boy from the ensemble was already there. With confidence, he walked around the cafeteria with a glass of sweetened black tea on his tray. He went through check-out and proudly walked away with one glass of tea and four bags of candies.

'Aren't you going to eat anything?' I asked him.

'No, I'm not that hungry.'

He smiled.

With the Years, My Passion for Music Only Grew and I Still Dreamed of Becoming an Opera Singer

On the radio, I often heard opera soprano star Inese Galante. My mother once told me that the singer's father had wanted a son and so she decided to work as hard as she could to make her father proud of having a daughter. I had no way to check the truthfulness of the story but it inspired me to prove my worth to my parents through hard work. In the summer, while my mother and I were on the beach, I told her again and again that one day I was going to become an opera singer. My mother replied that opera singers need to be fat to make their voice powerful and loud. I looked around, saw a few curvy women walking along the beach, and decided that my dream was worth sacrificing my body. Since I had only heard her on the radio I didn't realise that Inese Galante, who inspired me to sing opera in the first place, was not fat.

I was so persistent about my wish to study music that my parents finally signed me up for an entrance exam at the music school. On the day of admissions, we entered a little old wooden house in the centre of Riga. First, I had to sing a song, then somebody else sang a melody that I had to repeat. Later, the same person clapped a rhythmical pattern and asked me to repeat it by clapping my hands. After evaluating my audition, the committee spoke to my father. They concluded that I had to do the preparatory course first but the preparatory course was so much more expensive than the regular studies at the music school that we couldn't afford it. There had to be a way out, and my father was determined to put his charm to use. After long negotiations, he made an agreement with the school director: I would be admitted directly to the first grade, and if I didn't progress fast enough, my parents would deregister me. I was over the moon.

Meet My Favourite Music Teacher

In the music school, every child had to choose one instrument as their specialisation. Since I was admitted under exceptional circumstances, I had no hand in choosing my instrument. By the time I was able to choose, all the groups were already full, and the only free spot that remained was in the cello class, which my mother then named "the leftover group". I was proud to have cello as my instrument and the day I met my cello teacher I even felt that I was lucky to have gotten that spot. I was mesmerised by her beauty and by how gentle and caring she was. With time, I got to know her better and I learned that she didn't have any children of her own; cello was her whole life. She loved her pupils and dedicated all her love and patience to them.

My parents took my music studies very seriously and so they didn't allow me to skip any practice sessions. My mother didn't help me with my regular school homework but she always found the time to sit through my cello classes and memorise all the things that the teacher told me to work on. At home, my mother came into the room regularly to check on my progress. If I didn't get something right, I had to keep on playing the cello until I could do it. At times, these practices were very frustrating, both for me and for my sisters as they had to witness my angry outbursts and screams in our shared room. When my teacher noticed long, thick vertical traces of dried out tears on my cello, she knew I had been struggling at home and she always knew how to make me laugh about it.

Sometimes after hours of practicing my mother sent my sisters to play outside, leaving me all alone with my cello. Through the open window I could hear my sisters playing and having lots of fun and that made me want to hurry up and finish my practice session. Then I failed even more. When my patience had completely run out, in anger I pressed the bow very tightly against the strings and made sound effects that reminded me of trees cracking in a storm.

The end of my first study year was approaching and I was preparing myself for the exam. Based on this exam the examination committee would determine whether I could continue my studies or whether I had to leave the music school for good. The day before the exam I was in the classroom with my cello teacher, playing the piece that I had been practicing. Then she suddenly stopped me and pointed to a bar in the score asking me to play that part once more. In every class, she played a melody on the piano and then I repeated it on the cello. I stared blankly at the score and saw my teacher's face turn pale. Less than twenty-four hours before my examination, she came to the frightening conclusion that over the course of the year I didn't learn the single most crucial thing; how to read a musical score, which was the main study material in the preparatory year. Instead, I had developed a strong musical memory. My teacher was in such shock that she begged me to not to tell anybody about it. After my cello exam, the next day, the committee commented that I was very musical and that I expressed the emotions and the message of the musical piece very well. I passed the exam and promised my cello teacher that I would learn to read notes over the summer break.

Reward System

In 1992, after finishing third grade at my elementary school, I was part of the group of smart kids who could skip an entire grade and jump directly to fifth grade. It was the last time the school offered the option to enter primary school a year early. That was also the year when the marking system in the entire country switched from the older system of five marks to a new system with ten as the highest possible grade. This new system was also applied in my music school and for a sweet tooth like me this was a very fortunate change.

Around the corner from my music school, a new ice cream cafe, "Penguin", had opened. That year I happened to get a very good grade in my cello exam. My cello teacher was proud of my performance and suggested to my mother that we go celebrate at the newly opened ice cream place. I ate one ice cream.

'Would you like another one?' my mother asked.

'Yes, of course, I'd love to!' I exclaimed.

And that's when my mother came up with a reward system for getting good grades in my cello exams; one ice cream for a seven, two ice creams for an eight, nine ice creams for a nine and ten ice creams for a ten.

Now that I knew what was at stake, my goals were clear. I played impeccably in my following cello exam and I became true entertainment for the Penguin vendors, who watched in disbelief as a ten-year-old worked down her tenth ice cream cone. That day I tried every flavour in Penguin ice cream cafe.

Every day when I came home from school my mother sat me down at my cello and I had to practice until it was bedtime. I had to play until my mother was satisfied with the result. Sometimes I was so frustrated that I cursed and screamed at her and in my thoughts I killed her. And I boiled with jealousy when I heard my friends talk about their after-school leisure activities.

Fortunately, all my fun-depriving hard work paid off and I was named the third best child cellist in the country in my age group. The day I travelled home with my prize diploma, I was met with a cake and the title "pride of the family". My parents were so obsessed with my success that I became a show-off item. In the light of my success, my sisters became completely invisible. I felt horrible for them but I was also enjoying the attention from my parents.

To acknowledge my success in the cello contest, my parents prepared another surprise.

One afternoon I came home, ready to do my homework, when my father walked up to me and casually asked, 'Would you be interested in a little trip to Germany?'

'What? To Germany? Of course!' I exclaimed.

'Well then, pack your bags, our flight is tomorrow morning,' he said.

When my sisters found out about the trip, they were very jealous.

The trip to Germany was my first flight to the west. We flew economy class which to my ears sounded like a special thing. We got a warm meal on the plane and the food was delicious, served in real ceramic dishes. After the main course, drinks and snacks kept on coming. All cutlery was made of stainless steel with an elegant Lufthansa logo on it. When I looked at the logo more carefully, I realised that I had seen a few of these same spoons at home. After the meal, my dad put one spoon in his bag.

'Dad, are you sure you can take it with you?' I asked him.

'Of course, I can. It's included in the ticket,' he said.

In Germany, I was startled by the abundance of everything. The shelves in the stores were full, the packaging was colourful and there was an arsenal of choice for any product you could imagine. In Latvia, the concept of supermarkets hadn't been introduced yet and I was surprised to find that the same store had not only food items but also clothes, books and bright neon plastic games and toys.

And then I came across the book section where I got myself something that I hadn't seen before; stickers with glitter. Up to that point I had only known about images that could be transferred to a surface by rubbing them with a wet cloth. After the trip, I brought my glittery stickers to school to show them to my classmates and suddenly everybody wanted to become my friend.

My stay in Germany was only a few days long. We went out to restaurants a few times and I couldn't believe the size of the portions. It is not an exaggeration to say that they were three times bigger than what I was used to eating. With hungry and fearful eyes, I looked at the plate, hearing my mother's voice in my head.

'No matter what's on your plate, you always have to finish it.'

Eating this portion felt like hard work. After swallowing the final bite, I felt as if everything inside and around my stomach was completely stuffed. My body hurt and I was unable to move. My father ended up carrying me out of the restaurant and straight into the car.

'Try to puke out the food,' he kept on repeating.

But I held back, as that would be too wasteful.

The next day was our flight back home. We waited for our plane in the lounge of the airport and there was so much food to look at that I started to get excited. I saw piles of bananas, luxurious sandwiches wrapped in plastic baggies, cookies, little packages of gummy bears and chocolate candies.

'Take what you want, it's free,' said my father and he stuffed his shoulder bag with bananas. I filled up my pockets with candies to surprise my sisters at home.

Visions

One day during the cello class my music teacher announced that the famous cellist Rostropovich was going to give a concert in Riga. My mother found the concert tickets expensive but she bought them anyway. Now that I was a prize-winner, these concert tickets were a form of investment into my professional future.

I loved the concert. Rastropovich's performance was impressive and the concert programme was amazing. The only thing that annoyed me were the geometric shapes that moved and jumped to the rhythm of the music in front of my eyes[25]. I had experienced similar visions in my music classes but in this concert the loudness of the symphonic orchestra made everything escalate. My mother asked me if I liked the concert, I told her that I liked it very much, but that the shapes were distracting me. I asked her what they were and she told me that I just had to ignore them. I listened to my mother, and no matter how persistent the visions were, I forced myself to chase them away and concentrate on the music instead. Over the course of time, these visions gradually faded away almost entirely.

The Rastropovich concert motivated me to work my hardest to sound great. At home, my professional career was still all my parents were talking about. They told me that if I was going to choose music as my career then I would have to transfer from my music school and the French lyceum to a professional music school. I loved this idea and my parents seemed to have accepted it.

Then one day something happened; my parents held a very long discussion in which my mother convinced my father to think about things differently. As she saw me as someone who was very clumsy, my mother believed that I would

---

[25] Fifteen years later, I found out that what I was experiencing was synaesthesia, and to my regret, all that's left of it now are short visions on rare occasions if a sudden loud sound occurs.

ruin my career the moment I slip on ice and break my arm. She used this argument to force me into choosing a different career. I guess she forgot that after years of swallowing fluoride pills my bones had most likely become indestructible.

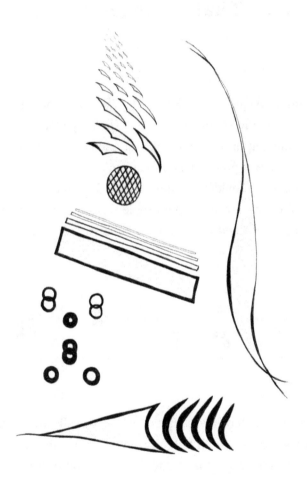

The Bs That Changed Everything

On the morning of August 23, 1989, my father left the house with his camera. He said he was going to fly in a helicopter. Then my mother told me that there were people gathering on Lenin Street, just around the corner from our house. We ran to see what was going on and found an astoundingly long line of people standing shoulder-to-shoulder, holding hands. I couldn't see the end of this human chain in either direction. The people welcomed us to join in. It was the notorious Baltic Way[26] and I became one little particle in this massive human chain.

In 1990, a concrete block was placed on the sidewalk around the corner from my house. It was covered with ugly drawings. I remember watching a bizarre scene where a man tried to climb it and there were joyful screams and applause from people passing by who watched him do that. When I asked my parents what was going on, they said something about a long-standing wall in Berlin that separated the east from the west and the destruction of the wall.

---

[26] The Baltic Way was a peaceful political demonstration held by approximately 2 million people who formed a 675.5 kilometre-long human chain spanning across the three Baltic states – Estonia, Latvia, and Lithuania, all three of which were then still under the Soviet occupation.

In January 1991, when I was seven years old, there were the Barricades[27] and tanks came to Riga. Schools were closed and everybody was urged to stay indoors. The anti-terrorist police OMON attacked my city with big armed vehicles. The people called them "Black Berets". My father sometimes left to film and then returned back home. It was a nerve-wracking time. My parents didn't explain much about what was going on and they had no idea how long this Black Beret thing would last.

Then one afternoon my father took us to Old Riga. He said he wanted us to see the Barricades, as it was an important event in Latvian history. He explained that the Black Berets were mainly inactive during the daytime – they couldn't pass with their tanks through the blocked narrow streets of Old Riga, so the only way they could move around was on foot on the ground or by climbing the rooftops.

On the day we saw the Barricades, it was very cold. My mother stayed home. All the streets in the old town were blocked with trucks, concrete blocks and big wooden beams. People were wrapped in thick winter clothes, peacefully sitting by the fire and guarding the Barricades. Everybody greeted each other. We went into the church to warm up. It was full of people in need of warmth and something to eat and drink. In the church my father walked towards a lady who was standing behind a portable electric stove. It appeared like she knew my father or maybe she was just very friendly to everybody. She was stirring a big pan and she asked if we wanted some tea. We said yes. The tea was delicious – it was made of apple jam diluted with water. I thought it was a very tasty alternative to plain black tea.

---

[27] The Barricades lasted from January 13 until January 27 in 1991. The events received this name because of people's efforts building and protecting barricades (mainly in Riga) to defend the targets that the Soviet OMON was attacking in attempts by the Soviet Union to regain control over Latvia.

We didn't stay long and we were home before dark. Later, reporters on the radio announced that there had been some deaths. In the evening, my father entered our room to wish us good night. He was already dressed, ready to go outside again and he was holding bags of film equipment. I remember it specifically because he usually didn't come to say good night.

My mother ran into our room and in a hysterical voice begged him to stay. She looked at us, seeking support to convince him to stay.

'If anything happens to you, I will have no way to raise three little children all by myself.' She sobbed. The next morning, we heard on the radio that two cameramen, Andris Slapiņš and Gvido Zvaigzne, who were documenting the events, had been shot. One died on the spot, the other died two weeks later from his wounds.

That night my little sister had a dream where she walked into my parents' room.

They were sitting on their bed looking out the window and they told her, 'Look, we have been shot.'

As they said that, they both showed their palms which had hockey pucks drilled into them with three little screws.

When the tanks finally left the city, our lives slowly went back to normal. Schools reopened. Our teacher asked us to bring a candle to commemorate those who had been killed during the Barricades. We joined a line of people on the street. I lit a candle to commemorate the victims of the Barricades and cried for my father's colleagues.

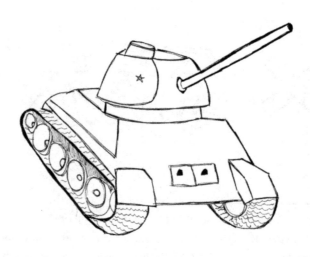

American Pen Pals and
Sonya's Lambada Skirt

After the fall of the Soviet Union in 1991, school uniforms were abolished from the educational system. More and more western goodies started to flow into Latvia and I quickly discovered a new problem with my habit of pressing my knees against the bottom side of a desk. My knees often got stuck on lumps of fragrant chewing gum. Chewing gum was still a luxury product that, by far, not everybody could afford. Some kids were so eager to chew it that they peeled it off from underneath the desk to give it a go. I knew from my early youth experiences that with the exception of Hercules, there's nothing more gross than cold saliva trapped in old chewing gum.

One Saturday afternoon, when my older sister arrived home after school, she brought home a package. She said it was shipped to her ballet school all the way from America.

'Who sent it?' we asked.

'My new American pen pal,' she proudly explained. 'A ballet school in America wants to start a friendship with our ballet school.'

The contents of the package were exciting. There was an orange velvet wallet with a zipper. One side of the wallet said FLORIDA. The word was written with black and white pearls and on the other side of the wallet there were two flamingos. Another item in the package was a nightgown with dark blue, light blue and white stripes. Fortunately, the pyjamas fit me better than my sister so I could keep them. We all referred to the pyjamas as "the earthworm". The most exciting gift in the package was a rectangular soft aluminium container filled with coloured pencils. We didn't care that they were already used. We were over the moon to see such an abundance of pencils, many of them in colours that no child in the Soviet Union had ever seen. There were pink pencils and purple pencils, orange pencils and different shades of green and blue. Inspired, we spent the rest of the day drawing.

My parents asked if we wanted to write something back and we were excited to do it. Then my parents came up with two little letters in English, one about my older sister and one about me. We made drawings with our new colourful pencils and we re-wrote the letters in our own handwriting. We never received reply.

My classmate Sonya also received a package from America and the entire school learned about its contents. Sonya's American aunt sent her a black lambada skirt and pink tights. While most of the children at school were still wearing a uniform (I surely did), or at the least a white blouse and a blue skirt or pants, Sonya showed up at school in her new American outfit. She could allow herself to have such a flashy look because she was an excellent pupil with excellent grades. Now that she had western clothes, everybody wanted to be friends with her. When the principal of the school approached her in the hallway, for a second Sonya thought she was in trouble. To her great surprise, the principal was so happy with her outfit that she asked Sonya if she could wear those same clothes and ring the bell to symbolically start the new study year on September 1, 1991. And that's what Sonya did. On the last day of August, Sonya's mother braided her long black hair, undoing the braids the next morning so that her hair would be curly and fluffy all day. After the Latvian national anthem and a speech from the director of the school, the most excellent pupil, Sonya Ivanova, rang the school's little bell. Her wild curly hair and lambada skirt gracefully floated in the wind.

Hangnail

In March 1991, the Popular Front of Latvia, a political organisation that dedicated itself to regaining independence, held a referendum calling on people to express their opinion about re-establishing the independence of Latvia. When he heard this call, my father stood in a long queue to send two telegrams to Moscow.

> 103062 Moscow, Chaplygin str. 3, to the representative of Latvia Mr Peters, message for the president of the USSR Mr Gorbachev = A genuine request to forget like our worst nightmare everything that has to do with you and the communist party = Mr Milbrets and his daughters

> 103062 Moscow, Chaplygin str. 3, to the representative of Latvia Mr Peters, message for the president of the USSR Mr Gorbachev = Leave us alone, or to put it another way, one cannot be loved by force = Cameraman Milbrets

Gorbachev did not send an answer to either of these telegrams. Much later my father did hear, however, that the KGB didn't appreciate reading his telegrams.

Monsieur Le Président

In 1991, Latvia declared its independence, and in 1992, President of France, François Mitterrand, was the first western leader to pay a visit to Latvia. Mitterrand also visited my school. Teachers and children prepared a full concert pro gramme with dance and songs especially for this occasion. Those with the best pronunciation of French were selected to stand in the front rows to shake the presidents' hand.

At the end of the day, me and a small group of my classmates found out that the French delegation's bus was still parked in the backyard of our school. When we went there to have a closer look, the bus was empty. We thought that we had the best chance to see our western guests if we stayed and waited right next to the bus. Shortly after, the delegation arrived. The door of the bus quietly opened. One French man disappeared behind the darkened windows. I thought to myself, *Missed chance, I should have said something to him.* Then he unexpectedly stepped back outside and gave me a pack of chewing gum.

To that I said, 'Merci beaucoup.'

At home, I told my parents what had happened and they beamed with pride at my French.

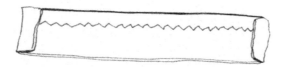

I Didn't Know How to Smile,
but I Did Find My Laugh on a Bus

In 1996, my music school was celebrating a big jubilee for which they were putting together a catalogue to showcase all the achievements of the students. A photographer was called in to take pictures of all the kids that had won musical competitions. He arranged the prize winners around a beautiful piano and took a photo. Then he looked at me and asked me if I could smile. With closed lips, I pulled my mouth into a smile and the photographer took a few more shots. After the photoshoot, another music school teacher took my hand and walked me to the mirror.

'Look how silly it looks if you smile without showing your teeth. You're messing up the catalogue!'

Later that year a recorder ensemble from Lyon came to visit my music school. At that time, I was already playing cello in the school orchestra. A special friendship concert was organised in a big concert hall. The programme of the night covered separate performances by the best students from my music school and the ensemble members from Lyon. We closed the concert beautifully, uniting as friends on stage and playing a few pieces all together. After the concert, there was a party to celebrate our friendship. Language was a barrier for starting conversations but playing games brought us closer. I was the only one in my orchestra who could speak French and I remember briefly chatting with a boy named Thierry, one of the youngest members of the recorder ensemble. He had curly hair and round glasses and he was so shy that our conversation dissolved very quickly.

After the concert, the recorder ensemble invited us to Lyon. And so, a few months later we travelled by bus for three days and two nights, waiting at every border for passport control until we finally arrived. Somewhere along the way to the west something magical happened. I suddenly broke into unstoppable laughter. It was loud and rhythmical and so contagious that everybody started laughing without even knowing what the joke was about. And as the entire bus was laughing I couldn't help but laugh even harder. Just the thought that people laughed without knowing the joke was so funny that it made me burst into even bigger peals of laughter. This was the first time I remember laughing and this became my signature laugh. It looked as if I was gasping for air, rocking back and forth in a way that made everyone else worry that I was having a seizure. I was having fun.

When we arrived in Lyon, it was dinner time. We all were ap pointed to a different family who drove us to their home and served us dinner. In my assigned family, everybody was quiet while eating.

Then after the main course, the mother, full of pomp and pride, brought a bowl and said to me in English with a strong French accent, 'These are cherries.'

To which I answered, 'Yes, I know, they grow in Latvia too.'

'Mother, she speaks French,' said her daughter.

At first, the mother was surprised but then she quickly concluded that French must be the language that is spoken in Latvia. She became curious about where I came from and brought out the atlas so she could try to find my country. The map was several years old and still had the USSR so I showed her the approximate location of Latvia on the map.

During this three week trip we gave concerts in various places and our orchestra earned money from the concert tickets. Our music school used this unexpected income to buy tickets to Disneyland in Paris. We had only a couple of hours to spend there before having to return back to Latvia. Those few hours in Disneyland left unforgettable impressions on me. I promised myself that I would visit it again one day.

Part III

The Fat Years and My Family's
First Luxurious Lunch

In the '90s, Latvia started booming and blooming, slowly becoming more Western. New opportunities for local and international businesses opened up and the Fat Years began. Latvia, now free and democratic, became a hotbed for show off culture. The number of cars on the streets increased and restaurants and cafes started popping up like mushrooms. They were a popular hangout place for businessmen in expensive suits. The first supermarkets were introduced making Western products like exotic fruits and juice in tetra packs available. With the Fat Years, access to colourful western clothes grew. Showing off wealth through physical appearance became essential; this was expressed through clothing and through the car that a person was driving. When the first McDonald's restaurant opened in Riga in 1994, it was advertised as the perfect place for a luxurious meal for a happy family. My mother looked down on McDonald's and she invented a new term, "McDonalder", which meant an uneducated loser.

My mother was very inclined towards emulating the life of intelligent and wealthy people and the Fat Years gave her the opportunity to reintroduce the aristocratic lifestyle that she had to suppress during our starvation period in Kommunalka. Now, as a bored and desperate housewife, she watched every episode of *The Bold and the Beautiful*, *Dynasty* and *Santa Barbara* and the next morning she watched their reruns. From time to time, she implemented things that she observed in these series in our family. Often when I came home from school, I found her still sitting in bed in her nightgown sipping champagne and eating luxurious nuts. She said that she was compensating for all the sacrifices she made to raise me and my sisters – her health, her good teeth and all the best years of her life.

During the Fat Years, my father built connections with the west which involved him getting into well-paid creative projects. More and more frequently he started travelling to the west and he came home from these trips with bags filled with coffee for my mother, western toys and treats for us, and of course lots of metallic cutlery from airplanes. For a couple of years, he worked very long days and through that he managed to save enough money to buy an old house with a piece of land around it.

This purchase was an unimaginable improvement after long years spent in poverty, feeling watched and squeezed in the overcrowded Kommunalka. When we moved to our new house, for the first time I felt no tension in the family. I even saw my parents hug sometimes. We were united, happy and excited to have a living space for just the five of us, with each of us even having our own door to close. Despite the poor condition of the house, which was worn down after years of serving as a Soviet Young Pioneer Camp, we decided to move in that summer, even before starting on renovations.

It was in this house that I remember the very first lunch my family had with all of us together at the same table. It was a warm, sunny day and we set a table on our veranda. My mother bought freshly baked white bread at the local bakery. We cut the bread into thick slices, spread a generous layer of butter and scooped a big spoon of the delicious cherry-plum jam that my father had made many years prior. I didn't even know we had so much jam. I guess my mother finally felt safe enough to use our family's Zakroma rodini stock.

The bread was fragrant and mushy and the crust was shiny and gentle on our gums. I observed how every bite I took of the bread left behind the clean-cut shape of my teeth. I admired the layers of three colours – white, yellow and dark orange – and watched a thin string of my saliva slowly stretch from my lips until it finally ripped. It felt as if I was eating cake. As I brought the slice of bread towards my mouth, the cherry-plums started to slide on the butter and thick sugary drops dripped down my hand, streaming to-wards my elbow. I took big chunky bites to save the plums from falling. I was savouring our wealth. After all, it was summer and my mother had finally allowed us to eat this liquid, sticky gold.

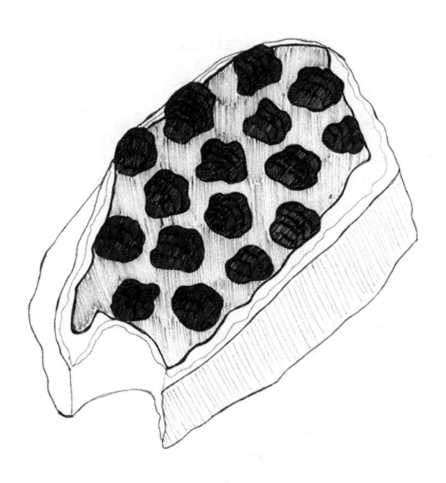

The Call Centre

The renovation works in our house started right after the summer and a year later we had already left the capital and started our life from scratch as wealthy people. Our house had two floors for just the five of us, and we all had our own individual room. It was only for a very brief period that my father was allowed to sleep in the master bedroom upstairs but during that period I felt like we were a united family.

Then one day my mother announced, 'I don't want that cold fat frog next to me.'

My father had indeed gained some weight. After decades of poverty, he was pretty much unstoppable when it came to eating. And I guess a lack of affection from my mother must have made him cold. To my knowledge, my parents didn't make any attempts to fix their romantic relationship after my father moved out of the bedroom – ever since this incident he lodged like a concierge on the couch in the tiny room next to the entrance in his own house.

We were spread apart through the house, which gave my father the idea to set up three phones; one in his room, one in the kitchen and one upstairs, on "the Lady's floor". This was a concept coined by my mother, most likely borrowed from *The Bold and the Beautiful*. In that series, she learned that wealthy people separate their private space, like the bedroom, from more public spaces like the living room. My father's room was on the public floor and he made it cosy in his own way by turning it into the head office of our own call centre. There was a couch on which my father rested, as well as a big office phone that had multiple functions; it was a phone, an answering machine and a fax. My father took on the full-time role of phone operator. If the phone rang, nobody was allowed to pick it up except my father. He was always expecting important phone calls, often from abroad. Even if I knew that somebody was going to give me a call, I still had to wait for my father to pick up the phone. Then he asked for the full name of the caller and shouted out who was calling and who had to pick up the phone. Once, when only me and my father were home, he broke the rule of "no access for men" and stepped foot on the Lady's floor.

I heard a knock on my door and my father's voice said, 'Phone call from Heaven.'

When he opened the door, I gave him a puzzled look. Then he continued smiling.

'A guy called Angel is asking for you.'

When my younger sister reached puberty, she started receiving phone calls more frequently. I already had some slight suspicions that sometimes my father monitored our phone conversations from his room and so I saved my most spicy girl-talk for the phone cabin on the street. My younger sister ended up learning this the hard way. Once she was on the phone, and right when she finished talking, my father called her to come downstairs. He gave her a lecture, and before she even tried to explain herself, he played her back a tape recording from her conversation. He had proof and thus he was right. He ended the lecture with his standard closing order, 'Disappear into your room.' When I came home later that day, my sister told me what had happened. I wasn't surprised that my father was listening to our phone conversations. I was more surprised that he had hacked his way into his answering machine so that he could use it as a recorder.

I could only speculate on why my father behaved this way, so instead I will talk about the grace with which my little sister handled this situation. After disappearing into her room, instead of feeling defeated, she came up with a way to get her revenge and she executed it like a pro. The day after the incident, while my father was outside, my sister went to the phone cabin on the street to make a call and leave a message on my father's answering machine. Then we both went into hiding on the Lady's floor, waiting for my father to come home. The front door opened and my father went straight to his room. As usual, he pressed the button on his answering machine and within seconds we all heard through the speaker a sleazy female voice commanding my father to 'Call me! 909-68-86, you have no choice, you will be my slave, you will do everything I order you to do, call me 909-68-86.' Shortly after, my sister went down the stairs and asked my father if there were any messages for her.

My father looked caught, quickly pressed the erase button and mumbled, 'No, no messages, only some girl practicing.'

If You Asked About the Most Embarrassing Moment of My Life, I Would Probably Tell You This Story

When my family had just moved into our new house, our neighbours found out that we came from the capital. That was a good enough reason to invite us right away to the birth-day party of their daughter, Magda. Me and my sisters were excited. It was the first birthday party I remember being allowed to attend. I went shopping for gifts with my mother and I was surprised with her generosity.

At 11:30, which was half an hour before the party, me and my sisters were already dressed and ready to go. All we had to do was open the gate of our fence, walk twenty meters and open the gate of the fence that leads to the garden of Magda's family house.

'It's impolite to show up too early,' said my mother. 'Besides, I want you to eat first. I don't want our neighbours to think that we don't feed you.'

And then my mother started cutting up veggies for a soup. I remember looking at the clock and feeling anxious.

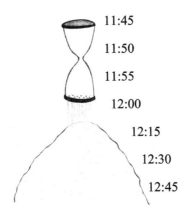

11:45
11:50
11:55
12:00
12:15
12:30
12:45

At 13:00, my mother served us soup. I ate it as quickly as I could.

'Don't rush it and chew properly,' she said.

The soup was followed by a main course. An unbearable feeling of embarrassment was growing in me. I was frightened to show up at a party more than an hour late. I had no appetite and I had lost my wish to party but just then my mother pushed us out of the house and sent us to our neighbours.

When we finally entered Magda's house, her mother walked us into the living room. The room was quiet, the table was full of bowls and dishes of untouched food. All the children were sitting around the table in complete silence waiting for the guests from the capital to finally arrive so that we could all sing the birthday song together, cut the birthday cake and start the birthday party.

One More Hairy Story

'There is hope,' said my mother one day when she came home from a hairdresser's appointment.

'Hope for what?' I asked.

Apparently, the hairdresser knew somebody just like me, someone whose hair hadn't grown in their early youth. Later, that person ended up with a full bushy head of hair.

By the time I was fourteen, everybody in my family could confirm that the hairdresser's prediction had come true – I had plenty of hair. Their ends were never trimmed, let alone cut. My older sister was still dreaming of becoming a hairdresser, even though she was dedicating her life to the noble profession of being a ballerina. In her free time, she practiced elaborate hairdos on my head. The strict ban on scissors didn't limit my sister. Instead, it only encouraged her to come up with workarounds and invent amazing hairdos that could be achieved with just braiding.

My long hair hung over my entire back. I couldn't handle its length nor its weight anymore. I finally rebelled and for the first time in my life I went to the hairdresser. In the evening, I turned up at home feeling an exciting adrenaline rush throughout my whole body. I knocked on my mother's door.

'Come in,' she responded.

I put a braid of my hair on her bedside table and said, 'Here, now my hair is safe with you.'

Family Photo Shoot

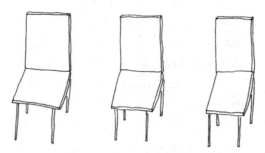

One night I was in my room doing my homework when suddenly my father called out our names and asked us to immediately come down. We unwillingly entered the living room, where we found three empty chairs set in one line in the middle of the space. My father's facial expression was somewhere in between anger and excitement. He held a camera in his hand and pointed at the chairs.

As soon as we took our seats, he started photographing us from different angles. Every now and then he giggled. My sisters and I looked at each other, puzzled. Then my father called out to my mother to come downstairs. He wanted her to witness this show.

My father continued taking the photographs.

'Let's see who will confess,' he said to my mother.

'Confess about what?' she asked.

Click, click.

'Come on, Dad, we have to do our homework,' me and my sisters said.

Then, in a split second, my father's face changed from mad laughter to furious rage.

In a low rumbling voice, he asked, 'Who broke the bathroom shelf?'

The three of us were quiet.

He took a few more individual and triple portraits.

'Come on, who will confess?' he continued. In the corner of my eye, I saw my mother quietly disappear into her room.

After a few more photographs and absolute silence from me and my sisters, he yelled at us, 'Disappear into your rooms!'

Later, at my father's birthday party, he took great pleasure in telling the story to his guests about how his spoiled daughters just wouldn't confess to breaking the bathroom shelf. He showed everyone our portraits and asked them to guess who might be the guilty one.

To this day my mother hasn't confessed.

Meet Alix, My First Western Friend

In 1999, I made a new Western friend. This time it happened through an exchange programme between my high school and the Lyceum of Balzac in Tours. Even though I wasn't directly involved in the programme, I ended up commuting to school every day for an entire week with Alix, an adorable and warm French girl with blue eyes. We clicked on so many levels that I soon realised that the differences in our cultural backgrounds didn't matter. It was as if we had already known each other for a long time. What I really loved about meeting Alix is that she gave me the feeling that the western world was filled with great opportunities, even for a girl like me.

The week flew by and sadly I couldn't be there on the day of Alix's departure. Heartbroken, I wandered around Riga that afternoon, until I bumped into a friend from my school. She said that Alix had written a letter for me and she had it with her. It was an adorable surprise that immediately lifted my spirits and deeply touched me. This letter was proof that Alix cared about our new friendship as much as I did. She had even attached a tiny earring that she had been wearing during her trip.

I was so inspired by this girl that I wrote her a long letter and sent it to France. She wrote me a long letter back and on top of that she also rewrote my letter with all my language mistakes corrected. As soon as I received her letter, I wrote her a letter back again.

Every time we corresponded; Alix rewrote my letters with all my mistakes corrected. I paid good attention to all these corrections and made notes in her letters of the expressions and words I didn't know yet. Sometimes I asked her language-related questions, and she explained the grammar rules as best she could, until one time she finally just sent me a grammar book. When I told Alix that I had to make a presentation about Corsica, she went straight to the tourist information centre and collected all the booklets that they had and she even found a tape that had samples of the native language of this French island. Thanks to Alix, I made a captivating presentation that would have been impossible without all that material (it would still be several years until the internet was easily accessible).

For years, we maintained contact as international pen pals. Through handwritten letters I got to know Alix much better; I learned about the things that were current in French teenage life and became more and more eager to discover the modern, open-minded and exciting Western world. I couldn't wait to dive into that world someday soon.

With Alix's dedicated help, my French improved rapidly. She was so proud of my progress that sometimes she read parts of my letters aloud to her family. Impressed with my writing, her parents even asked her to call me so they could shout "bravo" in unison. What a loving and supportive family they were. I was surprised at how involved they were with Alix's life and how much they cared about her friends.

Why I Have an Ozzy Osbourne CD

When I was sixteen, I had a crush on a boy who played the clarinet beautifully. He was so good at it that any music he played, no matter the composition, sounded heavenly. His performances revived my desire to give music a more important role in my life. I felt smart, serious, independent and responsible for my actions. I realised that I was old enough to have the ability to steer the course of my life towards my passion. My goal was clear; I had to make music my career. I didn't want to dwell on my frustration following my mother's decision to make me give up music.

I decided to start from scratch and pick a new instrument. I was determined to work my hardest and practice every day. At the first possible opportunity, I boldly approached the clarinet teacher in my music school. The old man had a friendly, warm smile and a good sense of humour, but nonetheless my heart was racing when I explained to him that I wanted to join his class. Children usually started playing wind instruments at the age of ten and I feared he would have to turn me down because of my age. But to my surprise he was happy to welcome a motivated girl amongst his pupils, although he advised me to choose the saxophone instead of the clarinet. He explained that the finger positions are the same on the two instruments but that the saxophone is much cooler for a girl like me.

I didn't care much about which instrument I learned – I got my second chance and I felt empowered by my own bravery. That same day I informed my parents about my decision to enter the saxophone class. Before they could even start to protest, I told them I was going to pay for the classes myself, although I didn't tell them I was going to pay for it with my lunch money. The only help I asked from my parents was for buying the instrument. Just before summer break, my teacher put me in touch with somebody who was selling a second-hand saxophone for a very low price. My father paid for it.

I couldn't wait for the new study year to start. The summer felt long. Every day I lifted my saxophone out of its case and held it in my hands. I didn't know yet how to play it but I was already in love with its shape, weight and shine. I pictured myself performing in front of big crowds. When the new study year finally started, I made sure to free up enough time to practice every day. My progress was fast and with it my *joy de vivre* returned. The boy who played the clarinet was a good friend of a good friend of mine. Over the summer my feelings for him didn't fade, so I tried to find a way to hang out with him. We spoke about music and about playing the clarinet and the saxophone. We were the same age but our playing levels were centuries apart. This difference only motivated me to work my hardest. Every practice session felt like a way to get closer to him and I daydreamed about us playing as a duo. I fell in love more and more with the boy until one day my feelings escalated. I had to let him know, so I wrote a let ter. It was a poem, with a summary of my romantic feelings in just one sentence in French in the Post Scriptum.

A day after sending the letter I received a phone call. It was him. My heart was racing. I was not prepared to discuss my feelings on the phone.

'Hey,' he said, 'I have a question.'

'Yeah?' I said.

'Could you help me out with something?' he continued.

'Sure, what's the matter?' I asked.

'So, I received a letter, and from the handwriting I can tell it's this girl in my class. She wrote me something in French and you are the only friend who could translate it for me.'

Nooooooooo, I was silently screaming in my head.

I felt paralysed. I hesitated about whether to tell him that I wrote the letter, but in my embarrassment, I chose to do what he asked. I translated the French sentence word by word in such a way that the poetic message didn't make any sense.

'Yeah, totally weird,' I added.

He was puzzled and then said that he kind of liked that girl. And if that wasn't painful enough, he asked me if I could give him some advice on how to approach her. That instant I was amazed at how a heart that's so broken could still keep on beating. I wrapped up the conversation quickly and after the phone call I forced myself to unlove the boy. I changed his role in my head from "my crush" to "my musical inspiration" and returned to hard practice; I never tried to find out more about him and the girl who wrote cryptic French in my handwriting.

One autumn evening I was playing the saxophone in my room when I noticed through the window that someone was waving at me. It was too dark to see details so I opened my window. Right outside my window was a big tree and behind it a big fence. When I asked who it was, from the answer I could tell I was talking to a stranger. I cannot recall the whole conversation we had but in essence the stranger wanted to say how cool it was that a girl played the saxophone (my saxophone teacher turned out to be right). The man sounded drunk and wouldn't leave. My only way out was to rudely cut the conversation short. I closed my window and carried on with my practice.

Half an hour later my father yelled up from the bottom of the staircase, 'There's a friend of yours downstairs waiting for you, come see him.'

'No, Dad, it's not a friend, I'm not coming!' I shouted back down from the Lady's floor.

Eventually, the stranger left. My father called me downstairs once again and pressed a CD into my hand.

'Here, he brought it for you,' he said in an angry voice.

'Dad, why did you let a stranger inside our house?'

My question made him so furious that he started accusing me of turning our house into a public walkthrough space.

'Disappear into your room!' he finally yelled at me.

I went upstairs, cleaned up, packed away my saxophone and took a look at the CD. *Ozzy Osbourne*, it said.

The next morning my father carried on with his regular daily routine. I avoided him as much as I could. Then I noticed that my younger sister didn't answer his "good morning". I didn't think much of it, but again the next morning she didn't talk to him, and again the day after that. Days passed, and soon she hadn't spoken to him for an entire week, and then for another week. The weeks of silence grew into a silent month and then that month turned into another month of no talking. In the end, my little sister gave him the silent treatment for one entire year. Years later, when I asked her about it, she said that this was her way to protest my father's accusations the night he let a stranger in our house.

You might wonder, how did my sister and my father come back to speaking terms?

One day my father was asking her something, my sister still refused to answer and he finally became so frustrated that he exclaimed in desperation, 'Why won't you talk to me?'

She didn't explain why, she just finally answered his previous question.

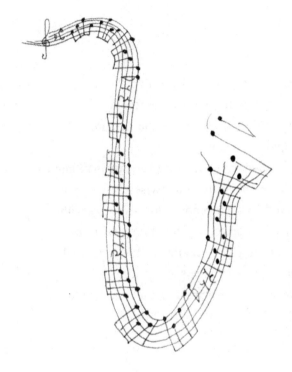

Five Loners

In my three years of high school, I felt like a misfit at the elitist Riga French Lyceum. I only shared my life with a few friends and my diary. Since my early youth, my parents had engraved in me the paranoid idea that "nobody can be trusted" and this applied to family as well.

By the time I reached puberty, we had grown apart into five loners who were united only by their last name and otherwise knew very little about each other. I even managed to work as a TV reporter for two years without my parents finding out about it. They only came close one time, when my father told me that our neighbour had seen me on TV. I replied that it's impossible.

My father said, 'Yes, I said the same to him.'

The less my parents knew about me, the less trouble it caused.

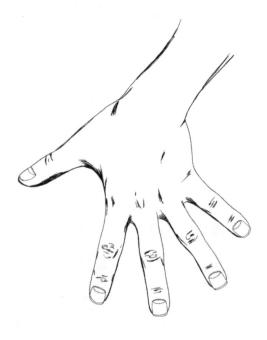

My Teacher's Birthday

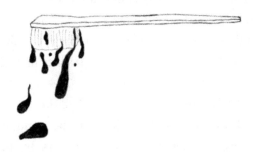

Just a few more days were left till the national saxophone contest, for which I'd been practicing for months. As part of the final preparations, my teacher scheduled an extra rehearsal. It was quite late in the evening and the streets were already dark and when I opened the doors to the music school my eyes were hit with a bright light. As usual, I entered my classroom to put down my things and prepare my saxophone. The tiny classroom space was empty. Instead of seeing my teacher sitting at his usual spot behind the desk, I found a beautiful bouquet of flowers that filled the room with joyful colours and scents. Behind the walls, just outside of the classroom, I heard a cheerful party. A familiar voice grew louder as it approached the door, and soon after my teacher walked in, announcing in a pompous voice that it was his birthday.

'Happy Birthday,' I said.

'Thank you,' he answered with a drunk smile on his face. 'Now I want a birthday kiss,' he said.

The old man was very dear to me – in the past he had supported me a lot and once when I came to class very hungry, he even offered me money to get myself some food.

'This money won't make you richer and it will for sure not make me poorer,' he'd said with a kind smile when he saw that I was reluctant to accept it.

He had a friendliness about him and a good sense of humour and he was so great at encouraging me that in some way he felt like family. Nevertheless, his request for a birthday kiss felt very odd and rather unpleasant but I didn't want to spoil the good vibes and I was in a rush to start the rehearsal. Unwillingly, I pressed a kiss on his cheek.

'That wasn't the kind of kiss I wanted,' he said.

My body froze as if venom had been injected into my veins. It was just the two of us in the tiny classroom and the door behind him was closed. I was trapped. I bit my teeth, unconsciously anticipating what was about to happen. He grabbed my ears with both hands and leaned towards my mouth. I felt his tongue sliding back and forth over my teeth. His breath smelled of alcohol. How the hell did I get myself into this situation? After my teacher had helped himself to a birthday kiss, he quickly took a step back.

As if the kiss had made him sober, he mumbled, 'I shouldn't have done this.'

Before we could say anything to each other, the piano teacher who played accompaniment for my piece entered the classroom, saying that the concert hall was ready for my rehearsal. My final rehearsal before the contest was a complete blur. I played all the notes robotically, and mutely nodded to all the final comments and tips that my teachers threw at me. All I could think of was brushing my teeth.

I don't remember how I got home but I remember frantically moving the toothbrush in my mouth. The moment I stopped brushing, the physical memory of the old wrinkly tongue sliding over my teeth and the smell of alcohol again invaded my mouth. I knew what had happened was wrong but embarrassment and doubts over whether I had provoked it started to take over my mind. I had no adult to turn to. For a fraction of a second, I considered telling my mother, who was home at the time, but I felt reluctant. I had so many reasons to not to trust her that every instinct I had held me back, trying to protect me. I could so easily picture our awkward conversation going in a direction where she told me that I provoked my teacher and that I brought it on myself and that was the last thing I needed to hear.

A few days after the incident, I gathered all my courage and took to the stage to play my heart out. At this performance, I let go of my dream, a dream that had been murdered by a venomous kiss. After my performance, I laid the saxophone in its case for long-term hibernation. I never turned up at my saxophone class again; I didn't want to face my teacher and most of all I didn't want to hear him say he's sorry. When my father found out that I had quit music school without finishing the study year, he only said, 'As always, I threw money out for your whim,' referring to the money he had spent to buy me the instrument.

Landing My First Paid Job

I was a first year student at the Academy of Culture when I found an announcement on the news board that called out to me.

CASTING
Summer job at Disneyland Paris
Age: 18+
Languages: French + another Western language

I had just turned 18 and thanks to Alix my French was very good. I felt like this offer was personally addressed to me and I went to the mass interview. There was a big group of enthusiastic students; nobody was scheduled for a specific time. Even though waiting for the interview to start seemed to take forever, the results were revealed right after each one. Most of the interviewed people were rejected and I started to feel discouraged about my chances. I was one of the last ones and I was one of the few who landed the job. I had an exciting summer ahead of me.

That summer I took an international bus to Paris along with two other girls who were going to work in Disneyland. Our bus arrived late in the evening and parked on a side street near La Gare du Nord. It was dark. From my study books, I knew Paris as the world capital of fashion and the city of love, I knew that France had an incredible history full of royalty and nobility and I knew about the French Revolution and Victor Hugo and the touching poetry of Baudelaire. What I didn't know was that there were also homeless people that piss on the street. The empty side of the station where our bus parked smelled like the boy's toilet in my old school. Close to our bus, a drunk man was shouting and kicking a vending machine. Me and the girls felt very unsafe. Before the trip, I had discussed everything with Alix and her brother had promised to come pick me up from the station. I looked for his car but didn't see it and a phonebooth was nowhere to be found. I didn't expect the station to be so immense. After walking around the area while the other girls waited for me and guarded my luggage, I didn't dare to keep looking for any longer. Both the other girls had a hotel reservation and they needed to check-in on time. They told me it was safer to go with them.

When we checked in the hotel, I was scared to bother Alix's family or my own parents with a late night phone call. In Paris, it was close to midnight and in Latvia it was even later. In order to make a phone call from the room, I had to make arrangements with the receptionist, who was already annoyed that we arrived so late. The girls insisted that I waited to call until the next morning.

When I got through to my family next morning, I instantly realised how stressed everybody was. Alix had called my father to say that her brother never met me. Hearing that, my mother immediately picked up a cigarette. I didn't realise she knew how to smoke – maybe she wasn't such an innocent hippie after all. After talking to my father, I was frightened to call Alix. When she picked up the phone, her voice sounded cold.

'My brother spent the night sleeping in the car waiting for you.'

I didn't know if it was anger or worry[28].

After these phone calls, me and the girls went to Disneyland, where we joined all the new employees in one big room. It was a nice introductory event and we all got a free entry ticket to the park. I went straight to Space Mountain, the only attraction I'd gone to when I was in Disneyland the first time.

As a Disneyland employee I had unlimited access to the park. For three months, I spent nearly all my free time visiting the attractions, either before or after my work shifts. I lived on the Disneyland campus, where I had no radio, no television and no other devices that could connect me with reality. I had no idea how to spend money properly or what a balanced diet actually meant. I ate white bread with butter and jam, as well as cereal with milk, like western people do and I enjoyed the freedom of coming home whenever I felt like it. My life was a fairy tale, until one day in September, on the bus to work, something felt off and I knew the fairy tale was over. When I reached the work canteen, I saw my colleague staring at a newspaper. On the cover, there was a photo of the Twin Towers exploding. At first, I assumed that a new Hollywood movie had been released. Later that day I overheard my colleagues having a conversation about

---

[28]A few days after that we managed to meet up and it was great seeing each other again. I was forgiven.

it and that's when this terrifying news from the outside world finally reached through my bubble. At midday, the entire park froze. The attractions, the music and the visitors all stopped and we joined each other in a moment of silence to commemorate those who lost their lives.

To me, the west had always been a symbol of freedom and democracy, where everybody is welcome and people are accepted for who they are, where all cultures live in harmony, where all dreams come true and everybody has equal opportunities. But after this event, everything changed. The garbage bins all disappeared and security started to patrol around the park, looking at everybody with suspicion.

Did I get to the west too late?

Advice from a Homeless Man

I finished my bachelor's degree at the age of twenty-one and suddenly I was an adult living back in Riga without a life plan. My temporary contract at a part-time office job was coming to an end and my applications for other office jobs were all turned down. My parents believed that all I needed for a successful career was a good diploma, and to the best of their knowledge, they had secured my future with good education. They thought that I wasn't getting hired because I was doing something wrong. In reality, I didn't even know what I was looking for. I had come to the frightening conclusion that at that point in my life everything I did literally fit on the same street; in the morning I walked to work and, in the evening, I walked back home. I was doing a job in which I saw no added value and I feared that all the other jobs I would ever have would turn out the same way. I couldn't bear the thought of a never-ending loop that kept spinning until I could retire. After years of studying hard, I expected a reward. I wanted an exciting life.

On one rainy day, I went to an internet cafe with my good old friend Sonya, whom I had known since first grade. Throughout the years she remained an excellent student and so my parents believed that Sonya was a very trustworthy person. Sonya also had no plan but she was ready for an adventure. We had both heard that some of our fellow students were applying for a translator course that would lead to a job opportunity in Brussels but that career didn't sound inviting to us. While I was browsing for volunteer jobs abroad, Sonya searched for study programmes in France.

Suddenly she exclaimed, 'Come here, look, I found a university for us!'

The university was in the suburbs of Paris, close to Disneyland and it offered two bachelor programmes; one for image and one for sound, which seemed to match both our interests perfectly. We submitted our applications and were admitted straight to the last year of the bachelor's programme.

My father put together all his savings and gave them to me, expecting me to educate myself in the west and to bring that knowledge back to Latvia. That was also my goal. A few weeks later, I embarked on the bus to France with one thousand euros in my wallet and a bag of clothes on my back. Sonya's budget was even tighter than mine. We departed on the same day but Sonya travelled as a hitchhiker. When I arrived in Paris, Alix's parents picked me up at La Gare Du Nord and this time I knew the exact spot where we would meet. They generously offered for Sonya and me to stay at their place for two weeks. Brave Sonya travelled the full distance to Paris, more than 1700 kilometres, in strangers' cars; it took her three days and two nights. At two o'clock in the morning, exhausted and smelling like burned wood, she crawled up next to me in bed.

In our first two weeks in France, Sonya and I had to find our own place to live. We didn't expect student accommodation to be as expensive as it was. We quickly realised that with our savings we wouldn't be able to survive longer than two months. We needed jobs. In the area around our university, weekend jobs were almost non-existent and in the off-season Disneyland wasn't hiring. With a stack of printed CVs, we went to the centre of Paris and handed them out like flyers in every cafe, bar and store. One afternoon while taking a break I joined a man on a park bench. We started chatting, he told me that he was homeless and I told him that we were struggling with finding a job. He told me that McDonald's had a policy of not turning anybody down.

A week later, I was filling-in an application form.

Age: 21
Previous job: Latvian Ministry of Education and Sciences
Career plans within McDonald's: None

Then we did our uniform fitting. While eating our free burgers with the other new employees, we watched the intro video, which featured an excerpt from *Pulp Fiction* about "Le Big Mac". After the film, we received our uniform and a printed work schedule.

To my surprise, in France I was perceived as good-looking and my dark Latvian hair was called blond. I was hired at the highest possible position for a new starter; I was a McDonald's hostess. I spent all my weekends wiping tables, filling up dispensers with napkins and straws, serving coffee and blowing up balloons for children's birthday parties. On my working days, I was contractually obligated to consume exclusively McDonald's food. When I came home, my hair, skin and clothes smelled of fries and my shoe soles were slippery from oil and mashed up bits of food.

Once, on a regular day at university, I found myself craving a burger. This surprised and terrified me – I had never had such cravings before. The only reason I ate that food was because of the agreement in the contract. It took me only a few months of eating McDonald's food to become addicted to it. That day I walked to the nearest McDonald's and ordered myself Le Big Mac. The kitchen employee put such a large amount of fatty mayonnaise on it that the flavour and texture of it almost made me throw up. The burger that I craved helped me snap out of my new addiction. From then on, I changed my work meals to a McDonald's salad, muffins and flavoured water.

Sonya and I always travelled to work together and our manager Zohra started a rumour that we were a lesbian couple. Zohra was especially rude and disrespectful to Sonya and it made me very angry. Once, when Zohra tried to use her managerial powers to humiliate me, I decided to give her a taste of her own medicine. I came very close to her, gave her a flirty smile and in a gentle voice said that I wanted to go out with her. She turned pale. Zohra was intimidated, and from then on, she stayed at a safe distance and avoided being in small spaces alone with me.

Working at McDonald's felt like exchanging hours of my life for survival money. Not only were some of my colleagues mean, but the clients were also disrespectful and rude, sometimes even going so far as to pinch my butt. After all, to them I was nothing more than an underachieving McDonalder. My East European background and my hair colour gave them the impression I was a worthless slut.

My mother liked to say, 'Cheese is only free in a mouse trap.' In some way, she was right. I got to enjoy a free education in France but at the cost of a miserable life. Making money was extremely difficult and even with all this hard work I was barely surviving. As I wiped down the tables at McDonald's, I repeated in my head my own personal survival mantra, 'You are here because of your dreams, you are here for a better life.' Then I caught a glimpse of my reflection in the mirror and saw an old woman trapped in a young girl's body. In this grim year, the only thing that kept me going was knowing that nobody forced me to be here, and if I wanted to, I could return to my country any time. Even though I had no money, I had my own two feet, and with them I could always walk home, even if it took a very long time. But I knew I had to fight for a better life in the west. Nothing and nobody was waiting for me back home.

Once More from the Top

After a rough year in France, I earned a new diploma but I still didn't feel any more prepared for adulthood. It was clear to me that I needed to buy myself more time. I craved a fresh start, where I could finally drop my past completely. That's when I decided to move to a place where I didn't know anybody and surround myself with a language that I didn't speak. I got admitted to the Royal Academy of Art in The Hague and I was determined to rediscover myself and come up with new dreams and goals.

Soon after the beginning of the study year, a poster in the hallway caught my attention. It was a call for musicians to perform a new piece using only toy instruments. Even though I hadn't set foot on stage for four years, for some unexplainable reason I felt drawn to this call and signed up. The day I went to the first rehearsal, the composer handed me a red plastic toy saxophone. I took a seat in the rehearsal space and started practicing my score. A few seats further down I noticed a young man with curly hair and round glasses playing a pink plastic recorder. His face reminded me of someone I knew.

'I'm sorry, can I ask you something?' I approached him in a hesitating voice.

The young man looked at me and stopped playing the recorder.

'Are you Thierry by any chance?'

'Yes, I am,' he answered in a tone of voice that almost sounded like a question.

'Years ago, we performed together when the recorder ensemble from Lyon visited Riga.' I prompted him.

'Yes, I was indeed in Riga,' said Thierry, but from his facial expression I could see that he didn't have any memory of meeting me.

On the day of our concert, I felt something very special about the two of us sitting on stage together. While Thierry was an aspiring professional musician, my life had taken me down a series of side paths, away from music. But for this one concert on the stage of the Royal Conservatoire we looked and sounded equally good. Playing an instrument that didn't look serious freed me from the fear of being judged because failing in this situation was impossible. The concept of this composition planted a seed in me – one day maybe I could invent my own musical instruments. Then I would be an artist, an inventor, an instrument builder and the only performer in the world who knew how that instrument sounds and how it has to be played.

And that's what I did to kill the demons from my past. Stepping off the path of a professional musician helped me to discover that I could live an even richer life by becoming an artist who creates my own world, a world that has no limitations.

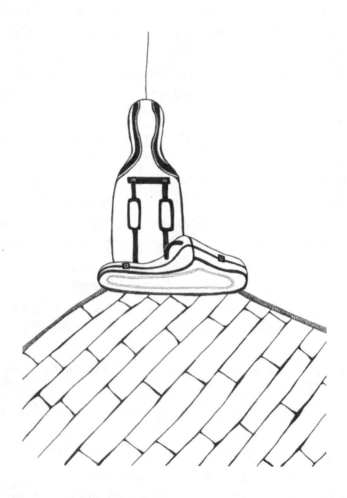

Afterword – How I Found Out That My Father Was Not Made of Aluminium

When the Soviet Union ceased to exist, the state distributed certificates to encourage people to privatise real estate. At that time, my father had already managed to buy the house in Jurmala but it still didn't match my mother's wishes. She wanted to own an apartment in the centre of Riga and she convinced my father to buy one. My parents went to visit apartments and then one day they announced to us that they had found one just a few blocks from Kommunalka. Ironically, it had also served as a communal house for other families during the Soviet Union.

We assembled all our family's certificates, to which my father added his last savings and with that we had just enough to buy that apartment. Because of this investment, my family was left with a tight budget for food and clothes. Unfortunately, the new apartment was so worn down that moving in directly was categorically not an option. This is why our parents announced that we were going to stay in our family house in Jurmala even after the summer holidays.

Even though it was obvious that we weren't going to move to the apartment any time soon, my parents made the decision to move the stuff that we had in Riga straight to the new apartment. Just as with all other important family matters, my sisters and I were left out of the process of moving. All that our parents asked from us was to keep quiet and disappear into our rooms. They assumed that none of us were capable of doing anything helpful for the family, though they never explained why or offered us a chance to prove ourselves. Instead, they called us lazy and spoiled.

My father took the task of moving upon himself. He boxed up all the family belongings that we had in Riga and stored them in the biggest room in our new apartment. He was so rushed that he didn't even have a chance to separate the useful things from the broken ones. Everything, including trash and dirty dishes, got moved. When he was finally finished, he put a lock on the door and left for Jurmala.

We never had enough money to finish the repair works in the apartment, including the room in which our stuff was stored. Twenty-five years later, my little sister finally received permission from my father to unlock this gate to our past. As she entered my family's encapsulated life from 1995, she found a massive jumble of things under a thick and sticky layer of dust. There were boxes with books and bundled newspapers. There were magazines and wall calendars. There were stacks of old curtains and linens. There were boxes full of other empty boxes and boxes with burned-out lightbulbs, paperclips, nails and screws. There were broken tools and jars with dried out paint. There were bags with tightly wound bits of rope and empty batteries (which needed to be saved, just in case). There were suitcases with unworn clothes that still had their Soviet price tags attached. There were empty coffee packs that me and my sisters used as lunch bags at school. There was the same set of furniture that was part of every Soviet household back in the times of Communist glory. There was a Christmas tree trunk and stand full of broken umbrellas. There were bags stuffed with empty plastic bags and packs of toilet paper with their Soviet wrapping still intact. There were our Soviet toys and table games. There were old perfume bottles, thirty-seven soap bars, five electric irons with degraded wire coating and our infamous Malutka. As if on a pedestal, on the highest tower of boxes, in honour of my mother's greatest gastronomic achievements, lay a filthy black frying pan filled with a thick layer of black-brown-orangish-yellow fat with a wooden spoon sunk in it that had not been touched for decades. There were all the things I had around me as a little child because my parents saved everything that they ever bought, never knowing what they might need during the darkest of days.

My sister lifted out and unpacked each box, bag and suitcase one by one, separating interesting things from trash. In one of the boxes that contained my mother's stuff, she found *The New Marriage Book, Marriage as a task of the present and the future*, published in 1971. When my sister flipped through the book, she quickly realised that our mother had loyally followed the Soviet advice of praising education and engaging in marital love activities only for the Soviet goal of growing the population. Then she put down the book and unearthed a modest black paper bag. In there, she found a stack of undated photographs.

My sister, like me, had always wished to have a photo album. She made herself a cup of tea and sat down to look through the pictures. She had never seen them before and was pleasantly surprised to realise that our father had, in fact, documented our childhood. There were photos of us at home and of the carefree days on our dacha. She found beautiful portraits of my sisters and I and even of some of our friends. There was a photograph of my mother holding a baby in her arms (my older sister, of course). This was a truly unique sight, as my mother never liked to have bodily contact with her children.

Amongst these photographs depicting my family's daily life, my sister also stumbled upon a photograph of a document. She almost skipped to the next picture but then she read the name on the document. It was not the name of anybody in our family. She took a picture of it with her phone and sent it to me. When I saw the document, I was startled. It was about a girl named Sandra. Oddly, she was born in the same year as me and she had ourlast name. When I read that my father was her father, my heart almost stopped. As a child I often imagined that I had a twin sister and I hoped one day to meet her. Who is Sandra? Is she really my twin sister? Is she alive? The document did not state her full date of birth, so I also thought Sandra might be my half-sister. Questions kept running through my head and with them were many possible answers. My little sister was as intrigued as I was.

'Next weekend I'm going to visit our father, so I'll just ask him about it,' she said.

A few days later she was at my father's house. She made herself a cup of tea, sat down on the comfy chair across from my father and said right away, 'Dad, I've been going through our family stuff and came across this photograph.'

She handed it to my father.

'Who is Sandra?'

My father's eyes glazed over when he saw the photograph.

He took a deep breath and finally said, 'We've been trying to hide it from you.'

After these words, everything fell silent for a long time.

He finally took an even deeper breath and continued, 'Your mother and I wanted to give her a beautiful name. When I went to register your sister, the employee that was issuing the birth certificate said that she could not put on the birth certificate a name that's not on the calendar. "A name that's not on the calendar is not a name. At home, you can call her whatever you want, but on paper she will be Sandra".'

My father took another deep breath and continued, 'Without hesitation the woman wrote Sandra on your sister's birth certificate. Day after day, for several weeks, I returned to the same office, insisting they correct the document. That didn't help, so I addressed several lawyers and even reached out to the Supreme Court.'

After hearing this story, I looked at my birth certificate and only now did I notice on the top right corner a modest stamp that says in capital letters "RE-ISSUED". The document that I was holding was in fact my second birth certificate. When I saw the date it was issued, I realised that – unlike my mother's version of the story, in which she claimed that I didn't have a name for two weeks – in reality it took my father four years and one month of pushing his way through a wall of bureaucratic red tape to finally get my name recognised. I phoned my father to find out more about it. In this conversation, he was shocked to hear that my mother had made me believe that he wanted a son.

'I was always happy with you as you are.'

We both cried.

My name was the biggest gift I got from him. This story also gave me a certain sense of pride in my father, who could not be bent by the Soviet regime.

.

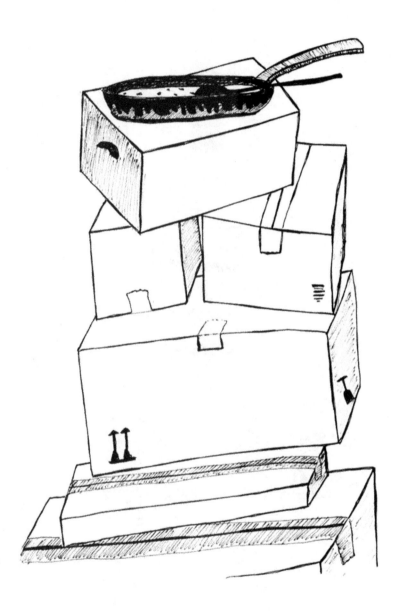

Gratitude

I would like to express my gratitude to those who raised me, educated me, grew up with me, studied and worked with me, made me become the person I am today and helped me in the process of creating this book. I thank all the characters in the book (the names have been changed, but you know who you are).

My fellow classmates at Riga French Lyceum; we went through all of this Soviet and post-Soviet madness together and we made it through!

My music school friends, especially the orchestra gang; even though we had to be very disciplined during the endless practices and rehearsals in the evenings and in the weekends, we also had so much fun on all our bus trips and concerts. And it makes me happy to see that most of you still pursue music.

I thank Dace Pūce for making me fall in love with the cello and for being a great mentor.

I thank my teachers at the Latvian Academy of Culture and my fellow classmates! These were four fun years spent not only being broke and still clubbing but also working as a team to process mountains of study materials.

I thank my fellow classmates at the Charles Cros Institute for welcoming me into your group. It is with you that my fascination for sound really sparked and I'm really proud and happy to see that many of you still pursue sound in your careers!

I thank my fellow classmates, colleagues and teachers at Art-Science / Interfaculty, especially Robert Pravda, who became my mentor even before I got one assigned. You were the first one I called when I was dumped and you told me to try them all. You were the first one I told when I found a new boyfriend and you told me that he's a very good choice.

La famille Jouve; Maman, Papa, ma soeur et mes frères, je vous aime! You are such kind and welcoming family.

And here comes my biggest gratitude, to the heroes who helped me in the process of creating this book; Cathleen Owens and Michael van Hoogenhuyze.

You were the first two people who believed in this project at its earliest stage and motivated me to carry on writing.

Austra Bērziņa, Kristīne Timma, Ilze Purmale and Jana Milbreta-Šmite shared their memories with me. Some of these details I have included in this book and thanks to your personal memories I remembered some of my own.

Senida Kalender, my little angel, you read my draft and prepared such solid feedback that we needed a two-hour phone call to talk it through. But I'm most thankful for your care and support and for convincing me about the importance of writing about my most painful and disturbing experience.

Victoria Douka-Doukopoulou, when you heard that I'm writing a book, you decided to shower me with must reads, amongst which was *Heating & Cooling* by Beth Ann Fennelly, which turned out to be the exact gem I needed to hold in my hands.

Santa Remere, you were not only my "call a friend" option for any quick fact check but you are one of my favourite people on the planet. Your ideas always fascinate me and your jokes make me laugh till I cry from belly pain.

Gaby Felten, after I showed you my first sketches, you encouraged me to illustrate my book myself. I've been applying your tips and filled this book with drawings thanks to you!

Stella Loning and Miranda Meijer, you asked me helpful questions and gave practical tips. Thank you!

I'm very grateful for inheriting an incredibly fancy office chair from Frits and Carry Kremer. It really improved my work conditions!

Maral Samir Gurbanzadeh, you helped me remember the exact Soviet terms and expressions in Russian, some of which I had only memorised in my child-language.

Thomas van Oortmerssen and Pete Martin, talking to you made me feel very excited about my own book. You unravelled a whole new way of looking at things and generously shared your golden knowledge and advice!

Who reads one book eight times and doesn't get bored with it? Susanna Bisschop, officially the only person that read all the drafts of my book. Wow!

I'm very grateful and pleased for all the detailed and helpful feedback from Theresa Owens, Kārlis Ozols and Maruta Voitkus-Lukins. You helped me understand how this book actually comes across.

Probably one of my biggest gratitudes goes to Ulla Milbreta – my little sister, who not only spent the last five years remembering with me the events from our past (I hope it was as therapeutic for you as it was for me), but also didn't hold back her cleaning urge during the first COVID-19 lockdown, unexpectedly supplying me with fascinating evidence just as I declared to my boyfriend the book as finally finished.

I send my love and gratitude to Andra Ādmine, who took such wonderful care of my dad in his final years. And cheers to you, Dad. I'm so happy that my writing briefly brought our family together. I'm happy you were finally ready for it. I hope you didn't feel interrogated when I knocked on your door with an intimidatingly long list of questions. I'm still impressed that you patiently answered all of them. I want you to know that I wrote this book because of you.

This book wouldn't read like this without a very fruitful collaboration with Tālis Saule Archdeacon. I've been excited about each and every meeting we had. It's been such a great learning process for both of us. Paldies! And I wouldn't have met Tālis if Yun Lee didn't offer me a slot for my performance during Bartalk.

I especially would like to thank the team at Austin Macauley Publishers for their trust, care, support and expertise in carrying out this book. And last but not least; I don't know how to thank enough Léon Spek, Zim and our cats Balsam and Pomelo – my boy gang, my biggest supporters and loves. The amount of patience you needed to find in the past couple of years is incredible as I was so often only physically present, while in my head I was floating in my book. But I have great news for you, and this time it is true; the book is finished!

The End

9 781398 465046